THE ULTIMATE PARTY DRINK BOOK

BRUCE WEINSTEIN

WILLIAM MORROW
An Imprint of HarperCollinsPublishers

In memory of my dad

L'chaim

THE ULTIMATE PARTY DRINK BOOK. Copyright © 2000 by Bruce Weinstein. All rights reserved. Printed in the United States of America. No part of this book may be used or reproduced in any manner whatsoever without written permission except in the case of brief quotations embodied in critical articles and reviews. For information address HarperCollins Publishers Inc., 10 East 53rd Street, New York, NY 10022.

HarperCollins books may be purchased for educational, business, or sales promotional use. For information please write: Special Markets Department, HarperCollins Publishers Inc., 10 East 53rd Street, New York, NY 10022.

FIRST EDITION

Designed by Jam Design

Printed on acid-free paper

Library of Congress Cataloging-in-Publication Data has been applied for.

ISBN 0-688-17764-6

01 02 03 04 / BP 10 9 8 7 6 5 4

THE

ULTIMATE

PARTY DRINK

BOOK

ACKNOWLEDGMENTS

WORKING on a cookbook is like going to a great party. There are always the thank-you notes afterward. Cheers to all!

At William Morrow—Justin Schwartz, my editor and friend. Carrie Weinberg and Corrine Alhadeff, my tireless publicists. Christine Tanigawa, Ann Cahn, Lorie Young, and the entire editorial production staff. Leah Carlson-Stanisic, Joann Metsch, Richard Aquan, Mary Speaker, and the entire design staff. Patrick Jennings, David Sweeney, and the entire sales staff.

At Writers House—Susan Ginsburg, my agent. Ann Stowell and Anne Wintroub, two extraordinary assistants.

At large—Patricia Clough, Felix Lao-Batiz, Andrew Mackhanlall, Bill Poock, and David Sisson.

At home—Mark Scarbrough. As always, thank you for—literally—everything.

CONTENTS

A BRIEF INTRODUCTION

Y OU don't need to be a professional bartender to make your party a success, and you don't need to learn how to make every drink ever invented. What you need are a few simple ingredients, a blender, a shaker, a pitcher, and some friends.

INGREDIENTS

LET'S start with ice. Size matters. The smaller, the better. Smaller ice cubes blend into smoother frozen drinks. Smaller cubes also have more surface area to quickly chill a shaken drink without watering it down.

The temperature of your ice matters, too. Right out of the freezer, ice is very hard. If you let it sit at room temperature for a few minutes before throwing it into your blender, the ice will soften and make a smoother drink. Just remember to drain off any water before using the ice.

Crushed ice is another way to ensure smooth frozen drinks. To crush ice without a machine, simply place your ice in a heavy plastic bag, seal it, and smash the ice with a heavy pot or pan. Drain off any water before using the crushed ice.

Blocks of ice are great for floating in pitchers and punch bowls. To ensure that the block of ice fits your punch bowl or pitcher, first make sure the container you use to make the ice fits inside your punch bowl or pitcher. For free-form ice, use watertight, plastic Ziploc bags. Don't fill them more than three-quarters full since water expands as it freezes. To remove the ice from the container or bag, dip it into hot water for a few seconds to loosen things up. Remember to drain any water before using the ice.

Fruit juices make blocks of ice and ice cubes that are both functional and pretty. Simply fill your container or ice-cube tray with the juice of your choice instead of water. Your drinks will stay cold without having their flavor diluted. Frozen fruit (such as strawberries or melon balls) also makes a decorative and functional addition to ice cubes, in both punch bowls and glasses.

Fruit and fruit juices are indispensable for making great party drinks. Unless otherwise indicated, use fresh fruit in your frozen drinks. Always smell the fruit before you buy it. If it smells sweet, chances are it is.

Many recipes in this book call for semifrozen fruit. To do this, simply wash, pit (if necessary), and slice (if required) your fruit, then place it on a plate in your freezer for an hour or so before making your drinks. The fruit should be icy but not solid.

Exotic and tropical fruit juices and nectars are showing up in stores everywhere. Flavors like youngberry, lychee, mango, banana, papaya, guava, guanabana, tamarind, passion fruit, red and black currant, pear, melon, strawberry, and peach are becoming as commonplace as orange and pineapple. A few good quality brands to look for include Ceres, Looza, Yoga, Goya, and Libby. If you can't find them in your local supermarket or gourmet store, they are available by mail from a number of very reliable sources, including Central Market in Austin, Texas (800-360-2552), Healthy Pleasures Village in New York City (212-353-3663), Dean & DeLuca in New York City (212-431-1691), and Whole Foods everywhere (800-780-3663).

If you are making drinks with alcohol, buy the best liquor you can comfortably afford. No amount of lime juice, passion fruit syrup, or sugar can hide the taste of cheap booze.

Fruit-flavored liqueurs are another important part of most mixed drinks. They come in a wide variety of flavors and prices. Your local liquor store owner should be able to help you choose the right ones to buy. It's important to remember that fruit-flavored liqueur is different from eau de vie. Eau de vie is a clear, distilled brandy with a lot of alcohol, a nice fruity aroma, but very little sugar and very little fruit flavor. Eau de vie is not on the ingredient list for most fruit-flavored drinks.

Fruit-flavored schnapps and liqueurs called "crème de . . ." are perfect for making fruit cocktails. For example, crème de banane, crème de cassis, and crème de framboise—they are all rich and sweet and, despite their names, contain no dairy. Fruit-flavored brandies are also very good for fruit cocktails. They are usually not as sweet as "crème de . . ." or other fruit liqueurs, but they do have plenty of fruit flavor.

Superfine sugar is called for throughout this book. It's available in most supermarkets. Sometimes it's called instant dissolving sugar or bar sugar. Unlike regular sugar, superfine sugar will never leave your guests with that "sandy" feeling between their teeth.

EQUIPMENT

GREAT party drinks need a good blender. I prefer those with narrow containers (about 4 inches in diameter). Some blenders come with containers an inch or two wider, and they act like mini food processors. They're great for pureeing soup but not for crushing ice into creamy drinks. The narrow blender pulverizes ice better, thereby creating smoother drinks.

For shaken drinks, you have a number of choices. You can use a basic metal cocktail shaker with a lid, or a larger metal bar shaker, which often comes with a second glass that fits on top and acts as a lid. This second glass is usually marked for measuring liquid ingredients in ounces.

If you don't have any shaker, you can always improvise. One way is to fill a pitcher halfway with ice, add the ingredients, and aggressively stir with a long-handled wooden spoon. Continue to stir until condensation appears on the outside of the pitcher. Then strain the drink into glasses filled with fresh ice. Or serve up (without ice) as the recipe indicates. I have also used a quart-size canning jar to shake drinks with nothing but my hand as the lid. This can get cold and messy, plus you need big hands. So if you choose to use a canning jar, use the lid the jar came with, or cover the top with plastic wrap then use your hand to seal the plastic in place while you shake the drink.

Whichever way you choose to shake your drinks, you will need to strain them afterward. You can buy a fancy bar strainer that fits the top of your shaker exactly, but the truth is, any small strainer will do in a pinch.

Measuring your ingredients in ounces is an important part of making great party drinks. If you don't have a shaker with the ounces indicated on the side, you can buy a two-sided cocktail jigger with a 1-ounce bowl on one side and a 1½-ounce bowl on the other. There is usually a halfway mark indicated on both sides to measure ½ ounce and ¾ ounce. If you don't have one of these, you can use a tablespoon. Just follow the Measurement Conversion Chart (page 5). All of these shakers, blenders, and strainers are available at hardware stores, kitchen stores, and most department stores.

For serving drinks, you'll find glassware in a wide variety of sizes, shapes, colors, and prices—martini glasses, margarita glasses, highballs, iced-tea glasses, wineglasses, balloon glasses, old-fashioned glasses, and more. Picking a glass is a no-brainer—use whatever you like, or whatever you have on hand. When I serve a drink that has a beautiful color, I prefer to use a clear glass. Other than that, pretty colored glasses make for festive parties. Some people like straws, some don't.

I always put a straw or a swizzle stick in my drinks and let my guests decide whether to use them. Just make sure that the straws and stirrers are long enough to fit the glasses you're using. It keeps your guests from having to fish them out.

The most important thing about making drinks is to have fun. And whether you choose to serve party drinks with alcohol or without, remember that aside from the company, a good drink is often the most memorable part of any party.

To help you know which drinks don't have alcohol and which do, simply look for a little martini glass with an *x* through it next to the name of the recipe. If you see one, you're still on the wagon. If not, there's booze in the blender.

MEASUREMENT CONVERSION CHART

½ ounce = 1 tablespoon

1 ounce = 2 tablespoons

1½ ounces = 3 tablespoons

2 ounces = ¼ cup

2½ ounces = ¼ cup plus 1 tablespoon

3 ounces = ¼ cup plus 2 tablespoons

3½ ounces = ¼ cup plus 3 tablespoons

4 ounces = ½ cup

4½ ounces = ½ cup plus 1 tablespoon

5 ounces = ½ cup plus 2 tablespoons

5½ ounces = ½ cup plus 3 tablespoons

6 ounces = ¾ cup

6½ ounces = ¾ cup plus 1 tablespoon

7 ounces = ¾ cup plus 2 tablespoons

7½ ounces = ¾ cup plus 3 tablespoons

8 ounces = 1 cup

BRUCE'S
FAVORITES

DRINKS FOR

EVERY OCCASION

During July and August, you'll probably serve piña coladas or frozen margaritas—both excellent choices. In December, you'll probably think eggnog, another perennial favorite. But what should you serve on Valentine's Day? Halloween? April 15? The fact is, we all throw parties all year long. Bachelor parties, bon voyage parties, Thanksgiving parties, New Year's Eve parties, Mardi Gras parties, Kentucky Derby parties, birthday parties, and more. Here are just a few of my favorite drinks to serve at some of these annual festive occasions.

AUTUMNAL EQUINOX
BLACKBERRY PEAR DAIQUIRI · 66

BABY SHOWER
LEMON CHEESECAKE THICK SHAKE · 53

BACHELOR PARTY
ZOMBIES FOR A CROWD · 164

BASTILLE DAY
FRENCH LEMON TWIST · 44

BIRTHDAY CELEBRATION (OVER 21)
BANANAS FOSTER COCKTAIL · 21

BIRTHDAY CELEBRATION (UNDER 21)
CHOCOLATE PEANUT BUTTER COOKIES AND CREAM SHAKE · 39

BON VOYAGE PARTY
THREE-HOUR TOUR · 127

BOOK GROUP
GRAPE GATSBY · 46

CHINESE NEW YEAR
DIM SUM SLING · 102

CHRISTMAS DAY
CHESTNUT SMOOTHIE · 31

CHRISTMAS EVE
COCONUT EGGNOG · 140

CHURCH SOCIAL
WATERMELON QUENCHER · 161

BLENDED

DRINKS

SLUSHES, SLOSHES,

SMOOTHIES, AND SHAKES

APPLE SUNDAE SMOOTHIE

MAKES 2 DRINKS

Canned apple pie filling works best for a drink that's smooth and sweet.

> 1 cup canned apple pie filling
>
> 1 cup vanilla ice cream
>
> ½ cup apple juice
>
> ⅛ teaspoon vanilla extract
>
> 3 ice cubes

Combine all the ingredients in a blender. Cover and pulse on and off until the mixture starts to swirl evenly. Blend on high for 20 seconds, or until the drink is completely smooth.

Variations

APPLE PIE SMOOTHIE Add 6 ginger snaps and ¼ teaspoon ground cinnamon before blending.

CANDY APPLE SMOOTHIE Add 2 tablespoons grenadine syrup before blending.

CARAMEL APPLE SMOOTHIE Add 2 tablespoons caramel topping before blending.

Spiked Variations

APPLE SUNDAE COCKTAIL Omit the apple juice. Add 2 ounces vodka and 2 ounces apple brandy before blending.

GINGER APPLE SUNDAE COCKTAIL Omit apple juice. Add 2 ounces vodka and 2 ounces ginger liqueur (such as the Original Canton) before blending.

APRICOT DAIQUIRI

Apricot liqueùr adds a rich apricot flavor to this drink, but you may substitute apricot brandy if you desire. The drink will taste stronger and won't be quite as sweet.

    2 cups ice

    ¾ cup canned apricot halves, drained and semifrozen (page 2)

    3 ounces gold rum

    2 ounces apricot liqueur (such as Apry)

    Juice of 2 limes

    2 teaspoons superfine sugar

Combine all the ingredients in a blender. Cover and pulse on and off until the mixture starts to swirl evenly. Blend on high for 20 seconds, or until the drink is completely smooth.

Variations

ALMOND APRICOT DAIQUIRI Omit the apricot liqueur. Add 2 ounces almond liqueur (such as amaretto) before blending.

CHERRY APRICOT DAIQUIRI Reduce the apricot halves to ½ cup and reduce the apricot liqueur to 1 ounce. Add ½ cup semifrozen (see page 2), pitted cherries and 1 ounce cherry liqueur (such as Heering) before blending.

HERBAL APRICOT DAIQUIRI Omit the gold rum and apricot liqueur. Add 3 ounces spiced rum (such as Captain Morgan) and 2 ounces herbal liqueur (such as Chartreuse or Strega) before blending.

LEMON APRICOT DAIQUIRI Omit the apricot liqueur and lime juice. Add 2 ounces lemon liqueur (such as Limoncello) and the juice of 1 large lemon before blending.

AVALANCHE

MAKES 2 DRINKS

As smooth and white as falling snow—but not as gentle. Watch out, or you'll get buried alive.

    2 cups ice

    1 cup vanilla ice cream

    2 ounces Irish cream liqueur (such as Baileys)

    2 ounces white crème de cacao

    2 ounces vodka

Combine all the ingredients in a blender. Cover and pulse on and off until the mixture starts to swirl evenly. Blend on high for 20 seconds, or until the drink is completely smooth.

Variations

BANANA AVALANCHE Omit the crème de cacao. Add 2 ounces crème de banane before blending.

MEXICAN AVALANCHE Omit the vanilla ice cream. Add 1 cup chocolate ice cream, ¼ teaspoon ground cinnamon, and ⅛ teaspoon almond extract before blending.

MINTY AVALANCHE Reduce the vodka to 1 ounce. Add 1 ounce peppermint schnapps before blending.

NUTTY AVALANCHE Omit the crème de cacao. Add 2 ounces hazelnut liqueur (such as Frangelico) before blending.

VANILLA AVALANCHE Omit the crème de cacao. Add 2 ounces vanilla liqueur (such as Licor 43) before blending.

BANANA DAIQUIRI

To ensure a creamy banana daiquiri, use a very ripe banana. Don't be afraid of a few brown spots. Inside, the fruit will be white and sweet.

> 2 cups ice
>
> 1 banana, peeled and broken into pieces
>
> 3 ounces gold rum
>
> 2 ounces crème de banane
>
> Juice of 2 limes
>
> 2 teaspoons superfine sugar

Combine all the ingredients in a blender. Cover and pulse on and off until the mixture starts to swirl evenly. Blend on high for 20 seconds, or until the drink is completely smooth.

Variations

BERRY BANANA DAIQUIRI Add 4 semifrozen strawberries (see page 2) before blending.

BUTTERSCOTCH BANANA DAIQUIRI Omit the sugar. Add 1 tablespoon butterscotch topping before blending.

CHOCOLATE BANANA DAIQUIRI Omit the sugar. Add 1 to 2 tablespoons chocolate syrup (according to taste) before blending.

ORANGE BANANA DAIQUIRI Reduce the crème de banane to 1 ounce. Add 1 ounce triple sec before blending.

SPICED BANANA DAIQUIRI Omit the gold rum. Add 2 ounces spiced rum (such as Captain Morgan) and 1 ounce cinnamon schnapps before blending.

BANANA MALT

MAKES 2 DRINKS

A small amount of ice makes this drink frosty without making it too slushy, while the bananas and ice cream keep it rich and smooth.

2 bananas, peeled and broken into pieces

1 cup vanilla ice cream

2 ice cubes

2 heaping tablespoons malted milk powder

½ cup milk

¼ teaspoon vanilla extract

Combine all the ingredients in a blender. Cover and pulse on and off until the mixture starts to swirl evenly. Blend on high for 20 seconds, or until the drink is completely smooth.

Variations

APRICOT BANANA MALT Reduce the number of bananas to one. Add ½ cup drained canned apricots before blending.

BANANA NUT MALT Omit the vanilla ice cream and vanilla extract. Add 1 cup butter pecan ice cream and ⅛ teaspoon almond extract before blending.

CHOCOLATE BANANA MALT Add ¼ cup chocolate syrup before blending.

COCONUT BANANA MALT Reduce the vanilla ice cream to ½ cup. Add ½ cup sweetened cream of coconut and 2 additional ice cubes before blending.

ORANGE BANANA MALT Omit the vanilla ice cream. Add 1 cup orange sherbet before blending.

STRAWBERRY BANANA MALT Add 2 tablespoons strawberry jam before blending.

BANANA MALT COCKTAIL Omit the milk. Add 2 ounces vodka and 2 ounces crème de banane before blending.

BANANAS FOSTER SMOOTHIE

Serve this after your next dinner party. After all, it's easier to make than the dessert it's named for.

½ cup ice

1 banana, peeled and broken into pieces

½ cup vanilla ice cream

2 tablespoons caramel topping

⅓ cup milk

Combine all the ingredients in a blender. Cover and pulse on and off until the mixture starts to swirl evenly. Blend on high for 20 seconds, or until the drink is completely smooth.

Variations

APRICOT BANANAS FOSTER SMOOTHIE Add 2 tablespoons apricot jam before blending.

BERRIES AND BANANAS FOSTER SMOOTHIE Add 6 strawberries before blending.

CHOCOLATE BANANAS FOSTER SMOOTHIE Omit the vanilla ice cream. Add ½ cup chocolate ice cream before blending.

COFFEE BANANAS FOSTER SMOOTHIE Omit the vanilla ice cream. Add ½ cup coffee ice cream before blending.

SPICED BANANAS FOSTER SMOOTHIE Add ¼ teaspoon ground cinnamon and a pinch of grated nutmeg before blending.

Spiked Variation

BANANAS FOSTER COCKTAIL Omit the milk. Add 2 ounces white rum and 1 ounce crème de banane before blending.

BERMUDA HIGH

Named after the weather phenomenon that keeps the Northeast steamy during the summer, this drink is the perfect way to bring the mercury down.

 2 cups ice

 ¼ cup tamarind nectar

 1½ ounces vanilla liqueur (such as Licor 43)

 1½ ounces blue curaçao

Combine all the ingredients in a blender. Cover and pulse on and off until the mixture starts to swirl evenly. Blend on high for 20 seconds, or until the drink is completely smooth.

Variations

BERMUDA CRUISE Increase the ice to 3 cups. Add 1 ounce white rum and 1 ounce crème de banane before blending.

BERMUDA LOW Increase the ice to 3 cups. Add 2 ounces coconut rum (such as Malibu) before blending.

BERMUDA SHORTS Increase the ice to 3 cups. Add 1 ounce spiced rum (such as Captain Morgan) and 1 ounce cherry liqueur (such as Heering) before blending.

BERMUDA TRIANGLE Increase the ice to 3 cups. Add 2 ounces gold rum before blending.

BRANDY ALEXANDER FREEZE

Perhaps the most classic of all brandy drinks, the Brandy Alexander makes a perfect transition from after-dinner cocktail to anytime party favorite.

2 cups ice

3 ounces brandy

4 ounces dark crème de cacao

¼ cup heavy cream, half and half, or milk (consult your cardiologist)

Ground nutmeg for garnish

Combine all the ingredients in a blender. Cover and pulse on and off until the mixture starts to swirl evenly. Blend on high for 20 seconds, or until the drink is completely smooth. Garnish with a sprinkling of ground nutmeg.

Variations

APRICOT ALEXANDER Omit the brandy. Add 3 ounces apricot brandy before blending.

BANANA ALEXANDER Reduce the crème de cacao to 2 ounces. Add 2 ounces crème de banane before blending.

BLACKBERRY ALEXANDER Omit the brandy. Add 3 ounces blackberry brandy before blending.

CHOCOLATE CHERRY ALEXANDER Reduce the crème de cacao to 2 ounces. Add 2 ounces cherry liqueur (such as Heering) before blending.

COFFEE ALEXANDER Reduce the crème de cacao to 2 ounces. Add 2 ounces coffee liqueur (such as Kahlúa) before blending.

HAZELNUT ALEXANDER Reduce the crème de cacao to 2 ounces. Add 2 ounces hazelnut liqueur (such as Frangelico) before blending.

RASPBERRY ALEXANDER Reduce the crème de cacao to 2 ounces. Add 2 ounces raspberry liqueur (such as Chambord or crème de framboise) before blending.

BUBBLE GUM BUZZ

This combination of fruit flavors and tequila tastes just like bubble gum. The only thing that makes it pink is food coloring. But it tastes so real, you might be blowing bubbles afterward.

3 cups ice

1 banana, peeled and broken into pieces

3 ounces gold tequila

3 ounces Cointreau

4 ounces crème de banane

4 ounces orange juice

Juice of 2 limes

2 teaspoons superfine sugar

2 drops red food coloring

4 pieces "soft" bubble gum for garnish

Combine all the ingredients in a blender. Cover and pulse on and off until the mixture starts to swirl evenly. Blend on high for 20 seconds, or until the drink is completely smooth.

If desired, garnish the edge of the glass with "soft" bubble gum.

Variation

You can add 2 drops of any food color you prefer, but change anything else in this drink and it just won't taste like bubble gum.

STRIPED BUBBLE GUM BUZZ Make the recipe without any food coloring. Pour half the drink into a small pitcher and add 2 or 3 drops of your choice of food coloring. Stir well. Add 1 drop of a different color to the drink remaining in the blender. Blend quickly to incorporate the color. Carefully spoon the different colors into a tall glass because if you pour them, you'll mix the colors.

CAMPARI FREEZE

Campari is a bitter Italian liqueur. Bartenders say that mixing it with orange juice is the best way to try it for the first time. This frozen version of Campari and OJ is guaranteed to hook someone at your next party.

1½ cups ice

1 cup orange sherbet

¼ cup orange juice

3 ounces Campari

1 ounce triple sec

Combine all the ingredients in a blender. Cover and pulse on and off until the mixture starts to swirl evenly. Blend on high for 20 seconds, or until the drink is completely smooth.

Variations

ORANGE NEGRONI FREEZE Omit the triple sec. Add 1 ounce gin before blending.

CAMPARI CITRUS FREEZE Omit the orange juice. Add ¼ cup grapefruit juice before blending.

CAPPUCCINO FROST

MAKES 2 DRINKS

Now you can make your favorite coffeehouse freeze at home!

2 cups ice

¾ cup milk

¼ cup coffee syrup

2 heaping tablespoons non-fat dry milk

1 tablespoon instant espresso powder

2 tablespoons superfine sugar

Combine all the ingredients in a blender. Cover and pulse on and off until the mixture starts to swirl evenly. Blend on high for 20 seconds, or until the drink is completely smooth.

Variations

ALMOND CAPPUCCINO FROST Add 1 ounce almond-flavored syrup before blending.

BUTTERSCOTCH CAPPUCCINO FROST Add 1 tablespoon butterscotch topping before blending.

CARAMEL CAPPUCCINO FROST Add 1 tablespoon caramel topping before blending.

HAZELNUT CAPPUCCINO FROST Add 1 ounce hazelnut syrup before blending.

MOCHACHINO FROST Add 1 tablespoon chocolate syrup before blending.

MOCHACHINO MINT FROST Add 1 tablespoon chocolate syrup and ⅛ teaspoon peppermint extract before blending.

RASPBERRY CAPPUCCINO FROST Add 1 ounce raspberry syrup before blending.

FROZEN CAPPUCCINO COCKTAIL Omit the coffee syrup. Add 4 ounces coffee liqueur (such as Kahlúa) and 2 ounces vodka before blending. This cocktail variation can be used as the base for all the other Cappuccino Frost variations.

CHERRIES JUBILATION

Call me old-fashioned, but I still serve cherries jubilee at dinner parties. So it seemed a natural to turn this delicious desert into a party drink. It's best made with fresh sweet cherries, but frozen will do in a pinch.

> 12 large, sweet cherries, pitted
>
> 1 cup ice
>
> ½ cup vanilla ice cream
>
> 1 ounce brandy
>
> 1½ ounces cherry liqueur (such as Heering)

Combine all the ingredients in a blender. Cover and pulse on and off until the mixture starts to swirl evenly. Blend on high for 20 seconds, or until the drink is completely smooth.

Variations

CHERRY PIE JUBILATION Add 3 crumbled graham crackers before blending.

CHOCOLATE CHERRIES JUBILATION Omit the vanilla ice cream. Add ½ cup chocolate ice cream before blending.

GRAND CHERRIES JUBILATION Omit the brandy. Add 1 ounce Grand Marnier before blending.

NUTTY CHERRY JUBILATION Add ½ ounce almond liqueur (such as crème de noya or amaretto) before blending.

SPICED CHERRIES JUBILATION Add ½ ounce ginger liqueur (such as the Original Canton) before blending.

Zero-Proof Variation

CHERRY JUBILEE SMOOTHIE Omit the brandy and cherry liqueur. Add 2 ounces cherry syrup and ½ teaspoon artificial rum flavor (optional) before blending.

CHERRY DAIQUIRI

Frozen cherries work just fine for this drink. Allow them to sit at room temperature for 10 minutes before using them. If you use fresh cherries, you'll need to pit them first.

- 2 cups ice
- ¾ cup pitted, sweet red cherries, semifrozen (page 2)
- 2 teaspoons superfine sugar
- 3 ounces white rum
- 2 ounces cherry liqueur (such as Heering)
- Juice of 2 limes

Combine all the ingredients in a blender. Cover and pulse on and off until the mixture starts to swirl evenly. Blend on high for 20 seconds, or until the drink is completely smooth.

Variations

CHERRY VANILLA DAIQUIRI Omit the sugar. Add 2 tablespoons vanilla syrup before blending.

CHOCOLATE CHERRY DAIQUIRI Omit the cherry liqueur. Add 2 ounces white crème de cacao before blending.

SOUR CHERRY DAIQUIRI Use sour cherries instead of sweet cherries.

SPICED CHERRY DAIQUIRI Omit the white rum. Add 3 ounces spiced rum (such as Captain Morgan) and ¼ teaspoon ground cinnamon before blending.

TROPICAL CHERRY DAIQUIRI Omit the white rum. Add 3 ounces coconut rum (such as Malibu) before blending.

WHITE CHERRY DAIQUIRI Omit the red cherries and cherry liqueur. Add ¾ cup pitted, white cherries (sometimes called Queen Anne cherries), 2 ounces kirsch, and 1 extra tablespoon superfine sugar before blending.

CHESTNUT CHILLER THRILLER

MAKES 1 DRINK

Perfect for a winter holiday party, New Year's Eve, or a touch of Christmas in July. Just remember to look for chestnuts packed in water or dry vacuum-packed. Candied chestnuts or chestnuts in syrup will make your teeth hurt.

> 1 cup ice
>
> ¾ cup vanilla ice cream
>
> ½ cup roasted, peeled chestnuts (fresh or canned)
>
> 1 ounce vodka
>
> 1 ounce hazelnut liqueur (such as Frangelico)
>
> 1 ounce vanilla liqueur (such as Licor 43)

Combine all the ingredients in a blender. Cover and pulse on and off until the mixture starts to swirl evenly. Blend on high for 20 seconds, or until the drink is completely smooth.

Variations

APRICOT CHESTNUT CHILLER THRILLER Add 2 pitted apricots (fresh or canned) and ½ ounce apricot brandy before blending.

CHOCOLATE CHESTNUT CHILLER THRILLER Add 3 tablespoons chocolate syrup before blending.

COCONUT CHESTNUT CHILLER THRILLER Omit the vodka. Add 1 ounce coconut rum (such as Malibu) before blending.

HERBAL CHESTNUT CHILLER THRILLER Omit the vanilla liqueur. Add 1 ounce herbal liqueur (such as Strega or Chartreuse) before blending.

IRISH CHESTNUT MINT CHILLER THRILLER Omit the vanilla liqueur. Add 1 ounce Irish cream liqueur (such as Baileys) and 1 tablespoon white crème de menthe before blending.

CHESTNUT SMOOTHIE

MAKES 1 DRINK

Since canned chestnuts are easy to find all year, this delicious smoothie doesn't have to be a winter-only treat.

$\frac{1}{2}$ cup ice

$\frac{1}{2}$ cup roasted, peeled chestnuts (fresh or canned)

1 banana, peeled and broken into pieces

$\frac{1}{4}$ cup unsweetened coconut milk

1 tablespoon honey

$\frac{1}{4}$ teaspoon vanilla extract

Combine all the ingredients in a blender. Cover and pulse on and off until the mixture starts to swirl evenly. Blend on high for 20 seconds, or until the drink is completely smooth.

 Variations

CINNAMON CHESTNUT SMOOTHIE Add $\frac{1}{4}$ teaspoon ground cinnamon before blending.

CRANBERRY CHESTNUT SMOOTHIE Add 1 tablespoon cranberry sauce before blending.

GUILT-FREE CHESTNUT SMOOTHIE Omit the coconut milk. Add $\frac{1}{4}$ cup skim milk before blending.

ORANGE CHESTNUT SMOOTHIE Add 1 tablespoon orange juice concentrate, thawed, before blending.

PEACH CHESTNUT SMOOTHIE Omit the banana. Add 1 small peach, pitted and sliced, before blending.

CHOCOLATE ALMOND OH JOY

A candy bar in a glass. Yum!

 1 cup vanilla ice cream

 ¼ cup milk

 2 ounces sweetened cream of coconut

 1½ ounces almond liqueur (such as amaretto)

 1½ ounces vodka

 2 tablespoons chocolate fudge topping (or chocolate syrup)

Combine all the ingredients in a blender. Cover and pulse on and off until the mixture starts to swirl evenly. Blend on high for 20 seconds, or until the drink is completely smooth.

Variations

BANANA CHOCOLATE ALMOND OH JOY Omit the almond liqueur. Add 1½ ounces crème de banane before blending.

MOCHA ALMOND OH JOY Omit the vanilla ice cream and almond liqueur. Add 1 cup coffee ice cream and 1½ ounces coffee liqueur (such as Kahlúa) before blending.

RASPBERRY CHOCOLATE ALMOND OH JOY Omit the almond liqueur. Add 1½ ounces raspberry liqueur (such as Chambord or crème de framboise) before blending.

 Zero-Proof Variation

CHOCOLATE ALMOND CANDY BAR SMOOTHIE Omit the almond liqueur and vodka. Increase the milk to ⅓ cup and add 1 ounce almond-flavored syrup before blending.

CHOCOLATE COOKIES AND CREAM COCKTAIL

This makes a perfect dessert, served with extra cookies on the side.

    1 cup chocolate ice cream

    ¼ cup milk

    1½ ounces white rum

    1½ ounces white crème de cacao

    4 chocolate cream-filled cookies, crumbled

Combine all the ingredients in a blender. Cover and pulse on and off until the mixture starts to swirl evenly. Blend on high for 20 seconds, or until the drink is completely smooth.

Variations

CHOCOLATE ALMOND COOKIE COCKTAIL Omit the crème de cacao and chocolate cream-filled cookies. Add 1½ ounces almond liqueur (such as amaretto) and 4 crumbled almond cookies before blending.

CHOCOLATE GINGERSNAP COOKIE COCKTAIL Omit the crème de cacao and chocolate cream-filled cookies. Add 1½ ounces ginger liqueur (such as the Original Canton) and 4 crumbled gingersnaps before blending.

CHOCOLATE PEANUT BUTTER COOKIE COCKTAIL Omit the chocolate cream-filled cookies. Add 4 crumbled peanut butter cream cookies before blending.

PECAN COOKIE COCKTAIL Omit the chocolate ice cream and chocolate cream-filled cookies. Add 1 cup butter pecan ice cream and 4 crumbled oatmeal cookies before blending.

VANILLA COOKIE COCKTAIL Omit the chocolate ice cream and chocolate cream-filled cookies. Add 1 cup vanilla ice cream and 4 crumbled vanilla cream-filled cookies before blending.

CHOCOLATE SOY SMOOTHIE

MAKES 1 DRINK

This delicious chocolate smoothie is perfect for your vegan and lactose-intolerant guests—or for anyone who just wants to avoid dairy.

    1 cup ice
    2 tablespoons peanut butter
    ½ cup soy milk
    ¼ cup chocolate syrup
    1 banana, peeled and broken into pieces

Combine all the ingredients in a blender. Cover and pulse on and off until the mixture starts to swirl evenly. Blend on high for 20 seconds, or until the drink is completely smooth.

Variations

ALMOND CHOCOLATE SOY SMOOTHIE Omit the peanut butter. Add 2 tablespoons almond butter and ⅛ teaspoon almond extract before blending.

CASHEW CHOCOLATE SOY SMOOTHIE Omit the peanut butter. Add 2 tablespoons cashew butter before blending.

CHEWY CHOCOLATE SOY SMOOTHIE Add ⅓ cup granola before blending.

CHOCOLATE MALTED SOY SMOOTHIE Add 2 tablespoons malted milk powder before blending.

VANILLA SOY SMOOTHIE Omit the chocolate syrup. Add ¼ cup vanilla syrup before blending. If desired, use vanilla-flavored soy milk.

CHOCOLATE TRIPLE THREAT

MAKES 1 DRINK

One kind of chocolate is never enough. This recipe calls for three, including hot cocoa mix. You may use any brand or flavor you like, including low-fat and sugar-free.

1 cup ice

½ cup chocolate ice cream

1 package hot cocoa mix (1-ounce size)

¼ cup chocolate syrup

½ cup milk

¼ teaspoon vanilla extract (optional)

Combine all the ingredients in a blender. Cover and pulse on and off until the mixture starts to swirl evenly. Blend on high for 20 seconds, or until the drink is completely smooth.

Variations

CHERRY CHOCOLATE TRIPLE THREAT Add 2 tablespoon cherry syrup before blending.

MALTED CHOCOLATE TRIPLE THREAT Add 2 heaping tablespoons malted milk powder before blending.

MEXICAN CHOCOLATE TRIPLE THREAT Add ¼ teaspoon ground cinnamon and 2 drops almond extract before blending.

QUADRUPLE CHOCOLATE THREAT Add 2 heaping tablespoons chocolate-flavored malted milk powder or chocolate-flavored Ovaltine before blending.

ORANGE CHOCOLATE TRIPLE COCKTAIL Decrease the milk to ¼ cup. Add 1 ounce Grand Marnier and 1½ ounces dark crème de cacao before blending.

QUADRUPLE CHOCOLATE COCKTAIL Decrease the milk to ¼ cup. Add 1 ounce vodka and 1½ ounces dark crème de cacao before blending.

RASPBERRY TRIPLE CHOCOLATE COCKTAIL Decrease the milk to ¼ cup. Add 1 ounce raspberry liqueur (such as Chambord or crème de framboise) and 1½ ounces dark crème de cacao before blending.

COCO-LOCO

Eighty proof positive that you cannot get too much coconut.

    2 cups ice

    2½ ounces coconut rum (such as Malibu)

    2½ ounces white crème de cacao

    2 ounces unsweetened coconut milk

Combine all the ingredients in a blender. Cover and pulse on and off until the mixture starts to swirl evenly. Blend on high for 20 seconds, or until the drink is completely smooth.

Variations

ALMOND COCO-LOCO Add 1 tablespoon almond-flavored syrup before blending.

BANANA COCO-LOCO Omit crème de cacao. Add 2 ounces crème de banane before blending.

HONEY COCO-LOCO Reduce the crème de cacao to 1½ ounces. Add 1 ounce honey liqueur (such as Bärenjäger) before blending.

LEMON COCO-LOCO Omit the crème de cacao. Add 2 ounces lemon liqueur (such as Limoncello) and 2 teaspoons sugar before blending.

MOCHO-LOCO Add 1 tablespoon coffee syrup before blending.

COLADA CON-NADA

MAKES 2 DRINKS

Put the pineapple in the blender first and this drink will blend more easily.

2 cups drained canned pineapple chunks (20-ounce can)

1/2 cup sweetened cream of coconut

3 cups ice

Combine all the ingredients in a blender. Cover and pulse on and off until the mixture starts to swirl evenly. Blend on high for 20 seconds, or until the drink is completely smooth.

Variations

APRI-CON-NADA Omit the pineapple chunks. Add 2 cups drained canned apricots before blending.

CINNAMON PINE-ORANGE CON-NADA Reduce the pineapple chunks to 1 cup. Add 1 cup drained canned mandarin orange segments and 1/4 teaspoon ground cinnamon before blending.

NUTTY CON-NADA Reduce the cream of coconut to 1/4 cup. Add 1/4 cup almond-flavored syrup before blending.

PASSION CON-NADA Reduce the cream of coconut to 1/4 cup. Add 1/4 cup passion fruit syrup or passion fruit concentrate before blending.

PLUM CON-NADA Omit the pineapple chunks. Add 2 cups drained and pitted canned purple plums before blending.

RASPBERRY CON-NADA Reduce the cream of coconut to 1/4 cup. Add 1/4 cup raspberry syrup before blending.

STRAWBERRY CON-NADA Reduce the pineapple chunks to 1 cup. Add 1 cup sliced strawberries and 2 teaspoons grenadine syrup before blending.

COOKIES AND CREAM SHAKE

MAKES 1 DRINK

This takes milk and cookies to a whole new level.

    ½ cup ice
    1 cup vanilla ice cream
    2 tablespoons vanilla syrup
    ¼ cup milk
    4 chocolate cream-filled cookies, crumbled

Combine all the ingredients in a blender. Cover and pulse on and off until the mixture starts to swirl evenly. Blend on high for 20 seconds, or until the drink is completely smooth.

 Variations

ALMOND COOKIES AND CREAM SHAKE Omit the chocolate cream-filled cookies and vanilla syrup. Add 2 tablespoons almond syrup and 4 crumbled almond cookies before blending.

CHOCOLATE PEANUT BUTTER COOKIES AND CREAM SHAKE Omit the vanilla ice cream. Add 1 cup chocolate ice cream and 1 tablespoon peanut butter before blending.

DOUBLE CHOCOLATE COOKIES AND CREAM SHAKE Omit the vanilla ice cream and vanilla syrup. Add 1 cup chocolate ice cream and 2 tablespoons chocolate syrup before blending.

DOUBLE VANILLA COOKIES AND CREAM SHAKE Omit the chocolate cream-filled cookies. Add 4 crumbled vanilla cream-filled cookies before blending.

GINGER COOKIES AND CREAM SHAKE Omit the chocolate cream-filled cookies and vanilla syrup. Add 2 tablespoons ginger-flavored syrup and 4 crumbled gingersnap cookies before blending.

S'MORES COOKIES AND CREAM SHAKE Omit the vanilla ice cream, vanilla syrup, and chocolate cream-filled cookies. Add 1 cup chocolate ice cream, 2 tablespoons marshmallow cream, and 4 crumbled graham crackers before blending.

CRANBERRY ORANGE SMOOTHIE

MAKES 1 DRINK

Who says cranberries are only for Thanksgiving?

1 cup ice

3 ounces orange juice concentrate, thawed

¼ cup whole cranberry sauce

1 cup vanilla yogurt (regular, low-fat, or non-fat)

1 banana, peeled and broken into pieces

1 tablespoon honey

⅛ teaspoon ground cinnamon

Combine all the ingredients in a blender. Cover and pulse on and off until the mixture starts to swirl evenly. Blend on high for 20 seconds, or until the drink is completely smooth.

Variations

CRANBERRY LEMON SMOOTHIE Omit the orange juice concentrate and honey. Add 3 ounces lemonade concentrate, thawed, before blending.

CRANBERRY PINEAPPLE SMOOTHIE Omit the orange juice concentrate. Add 3 ounces pineapple juice concentrate, thawed, before blending.

CRANBERRY WALNUT SMOOTHIE Add 2 tablespoons chopped toasted walnuts before blending.

CREAMSICLE SHAKE

MAKES 2 DRINKS

Premium ice cream will make the creamiest thickest shake, but lower-fat ice cream works—and you can even use non-fat ice cream or frozen yogurt.

> 1 cup ice
>
> 1 cup vanilla ice cream
>
> 1 cup drained canned mandarin orange sections (11-ounce can)
>
> ½ cup orange juice
>
> 2 tablespoons vanilla syrup

Combine all the ingredients in a blender. Cover and pulse on and off until the mixture starts to swirl evenly. Blend on high for 20 seconds, or until the drink is completely smooth.

Variations

CREAMY HAWAIIAN SHAKE Omit the mandarin oranges. Add 1 cup drained canned crushed pineapple before blending.

CREAMY PASSION FRUIT SHAKE Omit the orange juice. Add ½ cup passion fruit juice before blending.

CREAMY PEACH SHAKE Omit the orange juice. Add ½ cup peach nectar before blending.

CREAMY SUNRISE SHAKE Omit the mandarin oranges. Add 1 cup fresh blood orange sections before blending. Place 1 teaspoon grenadine syrup in the bottom of the glass before pouring in the shake. Streaks of red will rise beautifully up the sides of the glass.

CREAMSICLE COCKTAIL Omit the orange juice. Add 4 ounces vodka before blending.

ROYAL CREAMSICLE COCKTAIL Omit the orange juice. Add 2 ounces orange vodka and 2 ounces Grand Marnier before blending.

FIG AND HONEY SMOOTHIE

If you can't find fresh figs in your market, you can always order them through the mail from Harry & David (800-547-3033). Ask for Black Mission figs. They're dark purple and blend up into a beautiful lavender-colored drink.

> 4 large fresh figs (preferably Black Mission)
>
> ½ cup ice
>
> ¾ cup vanilla yogurt (regular, low-fat, or non-fat)
>
> 2 tablespoons honey
>
> Juice of ½ lemon (about 1 tablespoon)

Combine all the ingredients in a blender. Cover and pulse on and off until the mixture starts to swirl evenly. Blend on high for 20 seconds, or until the drink is completely smooth.

 Variations

DESERT FIG SMOOTHIE Omit the honey. Add 2 tablespoons tamarind syrup and 2 fresh, pitted dates before blending.

FIG AND APRICOT SMOOTHIE Omit the honey. Add 2 tablespoons apricot jam and ¼ teaspoon ground cinnamon before blending.

GINGER FIG SMOOTHIE Squeeze a 1-inch piece of fresh ginger in a garlic press to extract the juice. If the ginger is too large fit your garlic press, cut it into smaller pieces and repeat the process. Add ginger juice before blending.

LEMON FIG SMOOTHIE Use the juice of 1 whole lemon. Use lemon yogurt instead of vanilla yogurt.

FRENCH LEMON TWIST

Instead of taking your entire party to Paris, serve this thick, frosty libation and they'll arrive on the banks of the Seine.

    1 cup ice

    1 cup lemon sherbet, softened

    2 ounces vodka

    1½ ounces crème de cassis

Combine all the ingredients in a blender. Cover and pulse on and off until the mixture starts to swirl evenly. Blend on high for 20 seconds, or until the drink is completely smooth.

Variations

CHOCOLATE LEMON PEEL Omit the crème de cassis. Add 1½ ounces white crème de cacao before blending.

GREEK LEMON SQUEEZE Omit the vodka. Add 2 ounces ouzo before blending.

GREEN LEMON FREEZE Omit the crème de cassis. Add 1 ounce melon liqueur (such as Midori) before blending.

LICORICE LEMON SLUSH Omit the crème de cassis. Add ½ ounce anise liqueur (such as sambuca or Pernod) before blending.

WHITE LEMON FLURRY Omit the crème de cassis. Add ½ ounce white crème de menthe before blending.

FRUIT COCKTAIL COCKTAIL

This drink reminds me of my childhood. Not that I was having cocktails at ten, but the sweet flavor of canned fruit cocktail in any form sends me right back to second grade.

1 cup drained fruit cocktail (15-ounce can)

2 cups ice

2 ounces vodka

1 ounce apple schnapps

1 ounce peach schnapps

1 ounce triple sec

1 ounce cherry liqueur (such as Heering)

1 ounce sweetened bottled lime juice

Combine all the ingredients in a blender. Cover and pulse on and off until the mixture starts to swirl evenly. Blend on high for 20 seconds, or until the drink is completely smooth.

Zero-Proof Variation

FRUIT COCKTAIL SMOOTHIE Omit the vodka, apple schnapps, peach schnapps, triple sec, and cherry liqueur. Add ¼ cup peach nectar, ¼ cup apple juice, and 1 tablespoon grenadine syrup before blending.

GRAPE GATSBY

White grape juice concentrate is easy to find and keeps for weeks in your refrigerator, making this the perfect drink to whip up for unexpected company.

    2 cups ice

    2 ounces gin

    3 ounces white grape juice concentrate, thawed

    2 ounces pear nectar

    Juice of 1 lime

Combine all the ingredients in a blender. Cover and pulse on and off until the mixture starts to swirl evenly. Blend on high for 20 seconds, or until the drink is completely smooth.

Variations

ABSOLUTE GRAPE GATSBY Omit the gin. Add 2 ounces currant vodka before blending.

GREEK GRAPE GATSBY Omit the gin. Add 2 ounces ouzo before blending.

SICILIAN GRAPE GATSBY Omit the gin. Add 2 ounces grappa before blending.

GRASSHOPPER FROST

It's green, it's cold, it's delicious.

2 cups ice

1 cup vanilla ice cream

3 ounces vodka

2 ounces white crème de cacao

2 ounces green crème de menthe

Milk, as needed

Combine all the ingredients, except the milk, in a blender. Cover and pulse on and off until the mixture starts to swirl evenly, adding milk as necessary. Blend on high for 20 seconds, or until the drink is completely smooth.

Variations

ALMOND HOPPER Reduce the vodka to 1 ounce. Add 2 ounces almond liqueur (such as amaretto) before blending.

DOUBLE MINT HOPPER Omit the vanilla ice cream. Add 1 cup mint chip ice cream and 1 small, crumbled chocolate peppermint patty before blending.

FROZEN LOCUST Omit the vanilla ice cream and white crème de cacao. Add 1 cup chocolate ice cream and 2 ounces dark crème de cacao before blending.

FROZEN OREO HOPPER Add 4 crumbled chocolate cream-filled cookies to the blender, after the mixture begins to blend easily. Remember to add milk a little at a time if the mixture is too thick to blend.

MERRY CHERRY HOPPER Omit the green crème de menthe. Add 1 ounce white crème de menthe and 1 ounce cherry syrup before blending.

GUAVA GODDESS

MAKES 2 DRINKS

Fresh guava is hard to find in this country, and it's often expensive. Luckily, canned guava nectar is as sweet and delicious as the fresh variety when you're blending it up into a tropical treat.

2 cups ice

1/2 cup guava nectar

1 small peach, pitted and quartered

1/2 cup orange sherbet

2 ounces Southern Comfort

2 ounces vodka or orange vodka

Combine all the ingredients in a blender. Cover and pulse on and off until the mixture starts to swirl evenly. Blend on high for 20 seconds, or until the drink is completely smooth.

Variations

GUAVA A GO-GO Omit the vodka and Southern Comfort. Add 2 ounces white rum and 2 ounces crème de banane before blending.

GUAVA 'RITA Omit the vodka and Southern Comfort. Add 2 ounces tequila, 2 ounces triple sec, and 1 ounce sweetened bottled lime juice before blending.

 **Zero-Proof Variation**

GUAVA PEACH SMOOTHIE Omit the vodka and Southern Comfort. Add 1/2 cup orange juice before blending.

HONEYDEW DAIQUIRI

Make this drink with the sweetest melon you can find. Smell it before you buy it. Chances are if it smells sweet, it will taste sweet.

2 cups ice

1 cup honeydew balls or small cubes, semifrozen (page 2)

3 ounces white rum

2 ounces melon liqueur (such as Midori)

2 teaspoons superfine sugar

Juice of 2 limes

Combine all the ingredients in a blender. Cover and pulse on and off until the mixture starts to swirl evenly. Blend on high for 20 seconds, or until the drink is completely smooth.

Variations

FUZZY MELON DAIQUIRI Omit the melon liqueur. Add 2 ounces peach schnapps before blending.

HONEY HONEYDEW DAIQUIRI Omit the sugar. Add 2 teaspoons honey before blending.

LYCHEE HONEYDEW DAIQUIRI Add 4 drained canned lychees before blending. For a slushier drink, semifreeze (page 2) the drained lychees before making this drink.

MANGO MELON DAIQUIRI Omit the honeydew. Add 1 cup chopped mango before blending. For a slushier drink, semifreeze (page 2) the chopped mango before making this drink.

ORANGE MELON DAIQUIRI Omit the melon liqueur. Add 2 ounces triple sec before blending.

LEMONADE SLOSH

MAKES 2 DRINKS

All it takes is an easy-to-make lemon syrup to create dozens of delicious frozen lemonade cocktails that your guests will love.

2 cups ice

1 cup Lemon Syrup (page 51)

4 ounces vodka or lemon vodka

Combine the ingredients in a blender. Cover and blend until the drink is thick and smooth.

Variations

APPLE LEMONADE SLOSH Reduce the vodka to 2 ounces. Add 2 ounces apple schnapps before blending.

APRICOT LEMONADE SLOSH Reduce the vodka to 2 ounces. Add 2 ounces apricot brandy before blending.

BANANA LEMONADE SLOSH Reduce the vodka to 2 ounces. Add 2 ounces crème de banane before blending.

BLACK CURRENT LEMONADE SLOSH Reduce the vodka to 2 ounces. Add 2 ounces crème de cassis before blending.

BRITISH LEMONADE SLOSH Omit the vodka. Add 4 ounces gin before blending.

DIXIE LEMONADE SLOSH Omit the vodka. Add 2 ounces bourbon and 2 ounces Southern Comfort before blending.

DOUBLE LEMONADE SLOSH Reduce the vodka to 2 ounces. Add 2 ounces lemon liqueur (such as Limoncello) before blending.

GINGER LEMONADE SLOSH Reduce the vodka to 2 ounces. Add 2 ounces ginger liqueur (such as Canton) before blending.

MELON LEMONADE SLOSH Reduce the vodka to 2 ounces. Add 2 ounces melon liqueur (such as Midori) before blending.

MINTY LEMONADE SLOSH Add 2 teaspoons green or white crème de menthe before blending.

RASPBERRY LEMONADE SLOSH Reduce the vodka to 2 ounces. Add 2 ounces raspberry liqueur (such as Chambord or crème de framboise) before blending.

SLOE LEMONADE SLOSH Reduce the vodka to 2 ounces. Add 2 ounces sloe gin before blending.

 LEMON SYRUP

MAKES ABOUT 1 QUART

Easy to make, and it keeps for weeks—so double, triple, or even quadruple this recipe. (Just remember to use a larger saucepan.)

    2 cups water

    1 cup sugar

    1 cup lemon juice

Combine the water and sugar in a medium saucepan and place over medium heat. Stir until the sugar is dissolved and the syrup turns clear. Allow the syrup to come to a boil and let cook for 1 minute. Remove from the heat and allow to cool. Add the lemon juice and store in a covered container in the refrigerator.

LEMONADE SLUSH

This drink is the nonalcoholic version of Lemonade Slosh (page 50).

1 cup Lemon Syrup (page 51)

1 cup ice

Combine the syrup and ice in a blender. Cover and blend until the mixture is thick and smooth.

Variations

BLUEBERRY LEMONADE SLUSH Add ¼ cup blueberries before blending. For a slushier drink, semifreeze (page 2) the berries before making this drink.

MELON LEMONADE SLUSH Add ½ cup chopped melon before blending. For a slushier drink, semifreeze (page 2) the chopped melon before making this drink.

PEACHY LEMONADE SLUSH Add 1 peach, sliced and pitted, before blending. For a slushier drink, semifreeze (page 2) the peach slices before making this drink.

PINEAPPLE LEMONADE SLUSH Add ½ cup drained crushed canned pineapple before blending. For a slushier drink, semifreeze (page 2) the drained pineapple before making this drink.

PINK LEMONADE SLUSH Add 1 teaspoon grenadine syrup before blending.

STRAWBERRY LEMONADE SLUSH Add 4 to 5 semifrozen (page 2) strawberries before blending.

LEMON CHEESECAKE THICK SHAKE

MAKES 1 DRINK

No cream cheese. No eggs. No baking. Yet it tastes like cheesecake. Amazing. If you wish, use fat-free cottage cheese and fat-free frozen yogurt.

¼ cup lemon juice

½ cup cottage cheese

3 tablespoons superfine sugar

¼ cup vanilla frozen yogurt

1 cup ice

Combine all the ingredients in a blender. Cover and pulse on and off until the mixture starts to swirl evenly. Blend on high for 20 seconds, or until the drink is completely smooth.

 Variations

BLUEBERRY LEMON CHEESECAKE THICK SHAKE Add ½ cup blueberries before blending.

CRUSTY LEMON CHEESECAKE THICK SHAKE Add 2 crumbled graham crackers before blending.

GINGER LEMON CHEESECAKE THICK SHAKE Add 6 crumbled gingersnap cookies and ¼ teaspoon ground ginger before blending.

LEMON HONEY CHEESECAKE THICK SHAKE Omit the sugar. Add 3 tablespoons honey before blending.

SPICED LEMON CHEESECAKE THICK SHAKE Add 1 tablespoon poppy seeds and ⅛ teaspoon ground nutmeg before blending.

STRAWBERRY LEMON CHEESECAKE THICK SHAKE Add ½ cup sliced fresh strawberries before blending.

LHASSI FREEZE

MAKES 1 DRINK

While this Indian drink is refreshing, why ruin a party by telling your guests that it's also good for them?

1 cup ice

½ cup diced papaya (fresh or drained canned)

¼ cup orange juice

2 tablespoons honey

½ cup plain yogurt (regular, low-fat, or non-fat)

½ teaspoon orange flower water

Combine all the ingredients in a blender. Cover and pulse on and off until the mixture starts to swirl evenly. Blend on high for 20 seconds, or until the drink is completely smooth.

Variations

HOT LHASSI Add up to 1 teaspoon hot chili sauce (according to taste) before blending.

MANGO LHASSI Omit the papaya. Add ½ cup chopped mango before blending.

MINT LHASSI Omit the papaya. Increase the yogurt to 1 cup. Add 5 or 6 fresh mint leaves before blending.

SPICED LHASSI Add ⅛ teaspoon ground cardamom, ⅛ teaspoon ground coriander, and ⅛ teaspoon ground cinnamon before blending.

Spiked Variation

FROZEN LHASSI COCKTAIL Add 1½ ounces gin before blending.

MANGO SOY SMOOTHIE

MAKES 1 DRINK

Soy milk is available in most supermarkets and every health food store. It comes flavored and unflavored. I prefer vanilla-flavored. If you are allergic to soy, substitute rice milk.

1/3 cup soy milk (preferably vanilla-flavored)

1/2 cup mango nectar

1 cup ice

2 tablespoons apricot jam

1/2 banana, peeled and broken into pieces

Combine all the ingredients in a blender. Cover and pulse on and off until the mixture starts to swirl evenly. Blend on high for 20 seconds, or until the drink is completely smooth.

Variations

LITTLE SOY BLUE Add 1/2 cup semifrozen (page 2) blueberries before blending.

MANGO SOY MELBA Add 1/4 cup semifrozen (page 2) raspberries before blending.

STRAWBERRY SOY SMOOTHIE Add 6 semifrozen (page 2) strawberries before blending.

Spiked Variation

SOY SAUCE Add 2 ounces white rum or vodka to the main recipe or any of the variations.

MARGARITA FREEZE

If you like the taste of a margarita, you'll love this frozen version, which has little in common with the overly sweet convenience store slushes that pass for frozen margaritas in some chain restaurants.

    2½ cups ice
    4 ounces tequila
    2 ounces triple sec
    3 ounces sweetened bottled lime juice

Combine all the ingredients in a blender. Cover and pulse on and off until the mixture starts to swirl evenly. Blend on high for 20 seconds, or until the drink is completely smooth.

Variations

BANANA MARGARITA Add 2 ounces crème de banane and 1 banana, peeled, broken into pieces, and semifrozen (page 2), before blending.

BLUEBERRY MARGARITA Omit the triple sec. Add 2 ounces blue curaçao instead, and add ½ cup semifrozen (page 2) blueberries before blending.

CINNAMON ORANGE MARGARITA Add ½ cup semifrozen (page 2) orange sections and 2 ounces cinnamon schnapps before blending.

MELON MARGARITA Add ½ cup semifrozen (page 2) melon balls and 2 ounces melon liqueur (such as Midori) before blending.

RASPBERRY MARGARITA Add ½ cup semifrozen (page 2) raspberries and 2 ounces raspberry liqueur (such as Chambord or crème de framboise) before blending.

STRAWBERRY MARGARITA Add ½ cup semifrozen (page 2) strawberries and 2 ounces strawberry liqueur (such as crème de fraise) before blending.

MARSHMALLOW NUT FREEZE

MAKES 1 DRINK

Peanut butter and marshmallow cream are a classic combination that keeps adults eating (and drinking) like kids.

> 1 cup ice
>
> 2 tablespoons smooth peanut butter
>
> 2 tablespoons marshmallow cream
>
> 1/2 cup whole milk (low-fat or skim will work)

Combine all the ingredients in a blender. Cover and pulse on and off until the mixture starts to swirl evenly. Blend on high for 20 seconds, or until the drink is completely smooth.

Variations

MARSHMALLOW BANANA NUT FREEZE Add 1 banana, peeled and broken into pieces, before blending.

MARSHMALLOW CHOCOLATE NUT FREEZE Add 2 tablespoons chocolate syrup before blending.

MARSHMALLOW PEANUT BUTTER AND JAM FREEZE Add 1 heaping tablespoon either strawberry or concord grape jam before blending.

MARSHMALLOW RASPBERRY NUT FREEZE Add ¼ cup semifrozen (page 2) raspberries before blending.

Spiked Variations

CHOCOLATE MARSHMALLOW NUT COCKTAIL Add 1 ounce vodka and 1 ounce either white or dark crème de cacao before blending.

COFFEE MARSHMALLOW NUT COCKTAIL Add 1 ounce vodka or coffee vodka and 1 ounce coffee liqueur (such as Kahlúa) before blending.

VANILLA MARSHMALLOW NUT COCKTAIL Add 1 ounce vodka or vanilla vodka and 1 ounce vanilla liqueur (such as Licor 43) before blending.

MUDSLIDE

MAKES 2 DRINKS

Apoolside classic that whips up in a jif. That's good, because once you start making them, your friends won't let you stop.

1 cup ice

1 cup chocolate ice cream

2 ounces vodka

2 ounces coffee liqueur (such as Kahlúa)

2 ounces Irish cream liqueur (such as Baileys)

Combine all the ingredients in a blender. Cover and pulse on and off until the mixture starts to swirl evenly. Blend on high for 20 seconds, or until the drink is completely smooth.

Variations

CINNAMON MUDSLIDE Reduce the vodka to 1 ounce. Add 1 ounce cinnamon schnapps before blending.

COFFEE MUDSLIDE Omit the chocolate ice cream. Add 1 cup coffee ice cream before blending.

DOUBLE IRISH MUDSLIDE Omit the vodka. Add 2 ounces Irish whiskey before blending.

OREO MUDSLIDE Add 4 crumbled Oreos before blending.

TRIPLE CHOCOLATE MUDSLIDE Omit the coffee liqueur. Add 2 ounces dark crème de cacao and 1 tablespoon chocolate syrup before blending.

ORANGE JEWELIOUS

Afamous chain of juice joints made history with a creamy orange drink like this. A few still exist, but if you can't find one near you, you can always make a similar drink at home. The secret is the "magic" powder–instant pudding mix.

> 1 1/2 cups ice
>
> 1 cup orange juice
>
> 2 tablespoons vanilla syrup
>
> 2 heaping teaspoons instant vanilla pudding mix

Combine all the ingredients in a blender. Cover and pulse on and off until the mixture starts to swirl evenly. Blend on high for 20 seconds, or until the drink is completely smooth.

Variations

GRAPEFRUIT JEWELIOUS Omit the orange juice. Add 1 cup grapefruit juice before blending.

ORANGE CHOCOLATE JEWELIOUS Omit the vanilla syrup. Add 2 tablespoons chocolate syrup before blending.

PINEAPPLE JEWELIOUS Omit the orange juice. Add 1 cup pineapple juice before blending.

PINE-ORANGE BANANA JEWELIOUS Reduce the orange juice to 1/2 cup. Add 1/2 cup pineapple juice and 1 banana, peeled and broken into pieces, before blending.

STRAWBERRY JEWELIOUS Reduce the orange juice to 1/3 cup. Add 1 cup sliced strawberries before blending.

PAPAYA SMOOTHIE

Papayas should be golden, soft, and fragrant. Remember: The sweeter the fruit smells before you peel it, the sweeter it will taste.

> 1 medium, ripe papaya, peeled and seeded
> ¾ cup peach nectar
> Juice of 1 lime (about 2 tablespoons)
> 1 cup ice

Combine all the ingredients in a blender. Blend on high for 20 seconds, or until the drink is completely smooth.

Variations

GREEN PAPAYA SMOOTHIE Omit the peach nectar. Add ¾ cup white grape juice and 1 peeled, sliced kiwi before blending.

LATIN AMERICAN SMOOTHIE Omit the peach nectar. Add ¾ cup guanabana nectar before blending. Guanabana nectar is available in most Latin markets or by mail from Central Market (800-360-2552).

PACIFIC RIM SMOOTHIE Omit the peach nectar. Add ¾ cup white grape juice and 6 drained canned lychees before blending.

PAPAYA RAIN FOREST SMOOTHIE Add 2 tablespoons toasted cashew nuts, 2 tablespoons unsweetened coconut milk, and 3 tablespoons grenadine syrup before blending.

PAPAYA TAMARIND SMOOTHIE Omit the peach nectar. Add ¾ cup tamarind nectar before blending.

PEACH DAIQUIRI

MAKES 2 DRINKS

I never use canned peaches in this drink. They don't have enough flavor to make it as delicious as fresh or premium-quality frozen peaches. I also never peel my peaches. The little flecks of skin add texture and "eye appeal."

    2 cups ice

    1 large peach, pitted, quartered, and semifrozen (page 2)

    3 ounces gold rum

    2 ounces peach schnapps

    Juice of 2 limes

    1 teaspoon superfine sugar

Combine all the ingredients in a blender. Cover and pulse on and off until the mixture starts to swirl evenly. Blend on high for 20 seconds, or until the drink is completely smooth.

Variations

MINT-STREAKED PEACH DAIQUIRI Add 1 tablespoon green mint syrup or green crème de menthe to the glass before pouring in the daiquiri. The syrup will rise up in streaks along the sides.

PAPAYA PEACH DAIQUIRI Omit the peach. Add ¾ cup fresh or drained canned papaya cubes before blending.

PEACHARINE DAIQUIRI Omit the peach. Add 1 nectarine, pitted and sliced, before blending.

PEACHCOT DAIQUIRI Omit the peach schnapps. Add 2 ounces apricot brandy before blending.

PEACHY LYCHEE DAIQUIRI Add 4 drained canned lychees before blending.

PEACHY TEA PARTY FREEZE

MAKES 1 DRINK

Chillingly simple to make, this drink calls for iced tea mix sweetened with sugar. If you prefer to use sugar-free iced-tea mix, simply use the amount indicated on the package to make 2 cups.

1 cup ice

1 cup frozen peach slices

3 heaping tablespoons instant sweetened iced tea mix

1 cup lemonade

¼ cup water, as needed

Combine all the ingredients in a blender. Cover and pulse on and off until the mixture starts to swirl evenly. Add water, if needed, to get the mixture moving. Blend on high for 20 seconds, or until the drink is completely smooth.

Variations

BLUEBERRY TEA FREEZE Omit the peaches. Add ⅔ cup frozen blueberries before blending.

PEACH COBBLER TEA FREEZE Add 1 tablespoon hazelnut syrup before blending.

RASPBERRY TEA FREEZE Omit the peaches. Add ½ cup frozen raspberries before blending.

STRAWBERRY TEA FREEZE Omit the peaches. Add 6 frozen strawberries before blending.

Spiked Variations

DOUBLE PEACH TEA FREEZE COCKTAIL Omit the water. Add 2 ounces vodka and 1 ounce peach schnapps before blending.

EASY TEA FREEZE COCKTAIL Omit the water. Add 2 ounces vodka before blending.

PEACH MELBA TEA FREEZE COCKTAIL Omit the water. Add 2 ounces vodka and 1 ounce raspberry liqueur (such as Chambord or crème de framboise) before blending.

PEANUT BUTTERSCOTCH SHAKE

MAKES 2 DRINKS

This one will make everyone at your party feel like a kid in a candy store.

1 cup ice

1 cup butter pecan ice cream

2 tablespoons peanut butter

2 tablespoons butterscotch topping

¼ cup milk

Combine all the ingredients in a blender. Cover and pulse on and off until the mixture starts to swirl evenly. Blend on high for 20 seconds, or until the drink is completely smooth.

Variations

CHOCOLATE PEANUT BUTTERSCOTCH SHAKE Add 1 tablespoon chocolate syrup and 1 crumbled large peanut butter cup candy before blending.

PEACHY PEANUT BUTTERSCOTCH SHAKE Omit the milk. Add ¼ cup peach nectar and 1 peach, pitted and sliced, before blending. For a slushier drink, semifreeze (page 2) the sliced peach before making this drink.

PEANUT BUTTERSCOTCH AND JELLY SHAKE Add 2 tablespoons strawberry jam before blending.

Spiked Variation

PEANUT BUTTERSCOTCH COCKTAIL Omit the milk and butterscotch topping. Add 2 ounces gold rum and 2 ounces butterscotch schnapps before blending.

PEAR DAIQUIRI

Sweet, ripe pears are not always available when you need them, so I often use canned pears for this drink. I like to drain, then semifreeze them before making this drink.

2 cups ice

3 canned pear halves (8.5-ounce can), drained and semifrozen (page 2)

3 ounces white rum

2 ounces pear liqueur or syrup from canned pears

Juice of 1 lime

1 teaspoon superfine sugar

Combine all the ingredients in a blender. Cover and pulse on and off until the mixture starts to swirl evenly. Blend on high for 20 seconds, or until the drink is completely smooth.

Variations

ALMOND PEAR DAIQUIRI Reduce the rum to 1½ ounces. Add 1½ ounces almond liqueur (such as amaretto) before blending.

BLACKBERRY PEAR DAIQUIRI Reduce the rum to 1 ounce. Add 2 ounces blackberry brandy before blending.

CHERRY PEAR DAIQUIRI Add 6 maraschino cherries and 1 tablespoon of their syrup before blending.

HONEY PEAR DAIQUIRI Reduce the pear liqueur to 1 ounce and omit the sugar. Add 1½ ounces honey liqueur (such as Bärenjäger) before blending.

MINTY PEAR DAIQUIRI Add 2 teaspoons white crème de menthe before blending.

NUTTY PEAR DAIQUIRI Omit the the pear liqueur. Add 2 ounces hazelnut liqueur (such as Frangelico) before blending.

PEAR GINSENG DAIQUIRI Add one 10 milliliter bottle of ginseng extract before blending. Ginseng extract is available at most health food stores or by calling Central Market at (800-360-2552).

PEAR AND APPLE DAIQUIRI Omit the pear liqueur. Add 2 ounces apple schnapps before blending.

SPICED PEAR DAIQUIRI Omit the white rum. Add 3 ounces spiced rum (such as Captain Morgan) and ¼ teaspoon ground cinnamon before blending.

PIÑA COLADA

For a traditional flavor I like to use good-quality white or gold rum.

2½ cups ice

¾ cup pineapple juice

3 ounces sweetened cream of coconut

4 ounces either white or gold rum

1 teaspoon lime juice (optional)

Combine all the ingredients in a blender. Cover and pulse on and off until the mixture starts to swirl evenly. Blend on high for 20 seconds, or until the drink is completely smooth.

Variations

BANANA COLADA Reduce the rum to 2 ounces. Add 2 ounces crème de banane and ½ banana, peeled and broken into pieces, before blending.

CHOCOLATE ORANGE COLADA Omit the rum and pineapple juice. Add ¾ cup orange juice, 2 ounces Grand Marnier, and 2 ounces white crème de cacao before blending.

COBALT COLADA Reduce the rum to 2 ounces. Add 2 ounces blue curaçao before blending.

MANGO COLADA Omit the pineapple juice. Add ¾ cup mango nectar before blending.

MELON COLADA Omit the pineapple juice and reduce the rum to 2 ounces. Add ¾ cup white grape juice and 2 ounces melon liqueur (such as Midori) before blending.

PEACHY COLADA Reduce the rum to 2 ounces. Add 2 ounces peach schnapps and 1 sliced, pitted peach before blending.

SPICED VANILLA COLADA Omit the rum. Add 3 ounces spiced rum (such as Captain Morgan) and 1 ounce vanilla liqueur (such as Licor 43) before blending.

PIRATES' TREASURE

MAKES 2 DRINKS

In legend, pirates only drank rum. But had Captain Hook had a blender, he might have made one of these—and given Peter Pan a break.

2 cups ice

3 ounces spiced rum (such as Captain Morgan)

2 ounces vanilla liqueur (such as Licor 43)

1 kiwi, peeled and quartered

1 banana, peeled and broken in pieces

4 strawberries, hulled

Juice of 1/2 lime

Combine all the ingredients in a blender. Cover and pulse on and off until the mixture starts to swirl evenly. Blend on high for 20 seconds, or until the drink is completely smooth.

Variations

PIRATES IN PARIS   Omit the vanilla liqueur. Add 2 ounces crème de cassis before blending.

PIRATES IN TAHITI   Omit the spiced rum. Add 3 ounces coconut rum (such as Malibu) before blending.

PIRATES' SUNDAE   Reduce the ice to 1 cup. Add 1 cup vanilla ice cream before blending.

 **Zero-Proof Variation**

SOBER PIRATES   Omit the rum and vanilla liqueur. Add 1/3 cup orange juice and 1/4 cup vanilla syrup before blending.

PLUM PARTY FREEZE

This light, refreshing cocktail is a snap to make. With the addition of premium brandy and Grand Marnier, no one will ever guess you used canned fruit.

> 2 cups ice
>
> 6 canned purple plums, drained and pitted (15-ounce can)
>
> 1 cup drained canned mandarin orange sections (11-ounce can)
>
> 1½ ounces premium brandy
>
> 1½ ounces Grand Marnier
>
> Juice of ½ lemon

Combine all the ingredients in a blender. Cover and pulse on and off until the mixture starts to swirl evenly. Blend on high for 20 seconds, or until the drink is completely smooth.

Variations

APRICOT PLUM PARTY FREEZE Omit the mandarin orange segments. Add 6 canned apricots, pitted and drained, before blending.

CHRISTMAS PLUM PUDDING FREEZE Add 1½ ounces cherry liqueur (such as Heering), a few extra ice cubes, and ½ teaspoon ground cinnamon before blending.

CRANBERRY PLUM PARTY FREEZE Omit the mandarin orange segments. Add 1 cup canned cranberry sauce before blending.

CURRANT PLUM PARTY FREEZE Omit the brandy and Grand Marnier. Add 3 ounces currant vodka before blending.

PINEAPPLE PLUM PARTY FREEZE Omit the mandarin orange segments. Add 1 cup drained canned crushed pineapple before blending.

VIRGIN CRANBERRY PLUM PARTY FREEZE Omit the brandy and Grand Marnier. Add ⅓ cup cranberry juice before blending.

VIRGIN CURRANT PLUM PARTY FREEZE Omit the brandy and Grand Marnier. Add ⅓ cup black currant juice before blending.

VIRGIN ORANGE PLUM PARTY FREEZE Omit the brandy and Grand Marnier. Add ⅓ cup orange juice before blending.

PURPLE MANGO BONGO

MAKES 2 DRINKS

This refreshing blender drink has just a touch of Southern Comfort for flavor, but very little alcohol, so it won't bowl you over.

1 cup ice

1 small mango, peeled, pitted, and chopped (about 1 cup)

½ cup frozen blueberries

¼ cup apricot nectar

2 ounces Southern Comfort

1 ounce sweetened bottled lime juice

Combine all the ingredients in a blender. Cover and pulse on and off until the mixture starts to swirl evenly. Blend on high for 20 seconds, or until the drink is completely smooth.

Variations

PINK MANGO BONGO Omit the blueberries. Add 6 large frozen strawberries before blending.

RED MANGO BONGO Reduce the blueberries to ¼ cup. Add ¼ cup frozen raspberries before blending.

SUPER MANGO BONGO Add 1 ounce vodka before blending.

YELLOW MANGO BONGO Omit the blueberries. Add 1 cup frozen peach slices before blending.

 Zero-Proof Variation

MANGO BONGO SMOOTHIE Omit the Southern Comfort. Increase the apricot nectar to ½ cup.

RASPBERRY DAIQUIRI

Frozen raspberries are always available, always reliable. Take them out of the freezer about 15 minutes before you make this drink.

    2 cups ice

    1/2 cup raspberries, semifrozen (page 2)

    3 ounces white rum

    2 ounces raspberry liqueur (such as Chambord or crème de framboise)

    Juice of 2 limes

    1 tablespoon superfine sugar

Combine all the ingredients in a blender. Cover and pulse on and off until the mixture starts to swirl evenly. Blend on high for 20 seconds, or until the drink is completely smooth.

Variations

CHOCOLATE RASPBERRY DAIQUIRI Omit the raspberry liqueur. Add 2 ounces white crème de cacao before blending.

HAZELNUT RASPBERRY DAIQUIRI Omit the raspberry liqueur. Add 2 ounces hazelnut liqueur (such as Frangelico) before blending.

HONEY RASPBERRY DAIQUIRI Omit the sugar. Add 1 teaspoon honey and 1/2 ounce honey liqueur (such as Bärenjäger) before blending.

LEMON RASPBERRY DAIQUIRI Use lemon juice instead of lime juice. Add 1 ounce lemon liqueur (such as Limoncello) before blending.

PEACHY RASPBERRY DAIQUIRI Omit the raspberry liqueur. Add 2 ounces peach schnapps before blending.

RHUBARB DAIQUIRI

You'll need a batch of easy-to-make Rhubarb Elixir for this unusual drink.

- 2 cups ice
- 1½ cups Rhubarb Elixir (page 156)
- 4 ounces white rum
- Juice of 1 lime
- 1 teaspoon superfine sugar

Combine all the ingredients in a blender. Cover and pulse on and off until the mixture starts to swirl evenly. Blend on high for 20 seconds, or until the drink is completely smooth.

Variations

CHERRY RHUBARB DAIQUIRI Add ½ cup frozen cherries, pitted, and 2 tablespoons cherry liqueur (such as Heering) before blending.

RASPBERRY RHUBARB DAIQUIRI Add ½ cup frozen raspberries and 2 tablespoons raspberry liqueur (such as Chambord or crème de framboise) before blending.

STRAWBERRY RHUBARB DAIQUIRI Add 6 large frozen strawberries and 2 tablespoons grenadine syrup before blending.

Zero-Proof Variations

CHERRY RHUBARB SMOOTHIE Omit the rum. Add ½ cup frozen cherries, pitted, and 2 tablespoons cherry syrup before blending.

RASPBERRY RHUBARB SMOOTHIE Omit the rum. Add ½ cup frozen raspberries and 1 tablespoon grenadine syrup before blending.

STRAWBERRY RHUBARB SMOOTHIE Omit the rum. Add 6 large frozen strawberries and 2 tablespoons grenadine syrup before blending.

STRAWBERRY ALMOND BLAST

MAKES 1 DRINK

Strawberry lovers, your dream's come true. Strawberry juice is available at many grocery stores, most gourmet stores, or by mail from Central Market (800-360-2552) and Healthy Pleasures Village (212-353-3663).

1/2 cup ice

1 ounce vodka

1 1/2 ounces almond liqueur (such as crème de noya or amaretto)

4 frozen strawberries

1/2 cup strawberry ice cream

1/2 cup strawberry juice (see above)

Combine all the ingredients in a blender. Cover and pulse on and off until the mixture starts to swirl evenly. Blend on high for 20 seconds, or until the drink is completely smooth.

Variations

BANANA STRAWBERRY BLAST Omit the almond liqueur. Add 1 1/2 ounces crème de banane before blending.

CHOCOLATE STRAWBERRY BLAST Omit the almond liqueur. Add 1 1/2 ounces white crème de cacao before blending.

HAZELNUT STRAWBERRY BLAST Omit the almond liqueur. Add 1 1/2 ounces hazelnut liqueur (such as Frangelico) before blending.

LEMON STRAWBERRY BLAST Omit the almond liqueur. Add 1 1/2 ounces lemon liqueur (such as Limoncello) and 1 teaspoon grenadine syrup before blending.

MINTY STRAWBERRY BLAST Omit the almond liqueur. Add 1 1/2 ounces white crème de menthe before blending.

VIRGIN STRAWBERRY ALMOND BLAST Omit the alcohol. Increase the strawberry juice to ¾ cup and add ½ ounce almond-flavored syrup before blending.

STRAWBERRY DAIQUIRI

MAKES 2 DRINKS

A classic party drink you can serve any time of the year.

  3 cups ice

  7 to 8 large strawberries, semifrozen (page 2)

  3 ounces white rum

  2 ounces strawberry liqueur (such as crème de fraise)

  Juice of 2 limes

  2 teaspoons superfine sugar

Combine all the ingredients in a blender. Cover and pulse on and off until the mixture starts to swirl evenly. Blend on high for 20 seconds, or until the drink is completely smooth.

Variations

CHOCOLATE-DIPPED STRAWBERRY DAIQUIRI Omit the strawberry liqueur. Add 2 ounces white crème de cacao before blending.

DOUBLE BERRY DAIQUIRI Omit the strawberry liqueur. Add 2 ounces raspberry liqueur (such as Chambord or crème de framboise) before blending.

MINTY STRAWBERRY DAIQUIRI Add ½ ounce peppermint schnapps before blending.

ORANGE STRAWBERRY DAIQUIRI Add 2 tablespoons thawed frozen orange juice concentrate before blending.

PEACH STRAWBERRY DAIQUIRI Omit the strawberry liqueur. Add 2 ounces peach schnapps before blending.

TAHITIAN FREEZER BURN

Although this drink works with fresh papaya, it actually tastes better with canned fruit. Besides, canned papaya is easier to find and is usually less expensive. Remember to drain canned papaya before using the fruit.

 3 cups ice

 1 cup chopped papaya (fresh or drained canned)

 ½ cup papaya nectar

 ¼ cup lemonade

 2 ounces vodka

 1 ounce crème de banane

 1 ounce Grand Marnier

 1 ounce vanilla liqueur (such as Licor 43)

 1 teaspoon white crème de menthe

Combine all the ingredients in a blender. Cover and pulse on and off until the mixture starts to swirl evenly. Blend on high for 20 seconds, or until the drink is completely smooth.

Variations

TAHITIAN MANGO MIND BLOWER Omit the papaya and papaya nectar. Add 1 cup chopped mango and ½ cup mango nectar before blending.

TAHITIAN PEACH POWER Omit the papaya and papaya nectar. Add 1 large peach, pitted and sliced, and ½ cup peach nectar before blending.

 ## Zero-Proof Variation

TAHITIAN SUN SCREEN Omit all the alcohol. Add ¼ cup banana nectar, ¼ cup orange juice, and 1 ounce vanilla syrup before blending.

THANKSGIVING SMOOTHIE

MAKES 1 DRINK

Feeling like a little Thanksgiving in the middle of August? Why not serve up one of these smoothies. Canned yams make it easy and delicious. The only problem is you might be expected to deliver a turkey afterward.

2 ice cubes

1 cup drained canned yams

½ cup orange juice

½ cup pineapple juice

1 tablespoon vanilla syrup

Combine all the ingredients in a blender. Blend on high for 20 seconds, or until the drink is completely smooth.

Variations

CREAMY MAPLE THANKSGIVING SMOOTHIE Add ¼ cup plain yogurt (regular, low-fat, or non-fat) and 2 tablespoons maple syrup before blending.

ISLAND THANKSGIVING SMOOTHIE Add 2 ounces unsweetened coconut milk before blending.

THANKSGIVING CASSEROLE SMOOTHIE Add ¼ cup marshmallow cream before blending.

Spiked Variation

THANKSGIVING COFFEE COCKTAIL Add 1 ounce coffee vodka and 1 ounce coffee liqueur (such as Kahlúa) before blending.

VERY BERRY SMOOTHIE

MAKES 2 DRINKS

For the best results, keep the berries in the freezer for an hour or two before you make this drink.

> 1/2 cup blackberries, semifrozen
>
> 1/2 cup raspberries, semifrozen
>
> 1/2 cup sliced strawberries, semifrozen
>
> 1/2 cup blueberries, semifrozen
>
> Juice of 1/2 lemon
>
> 3/4 cup cranberry juice cocktail
>
> 1 cup ice
>
> 2 tablespoons grenadine syrup

Combine all the ingredients in a blender. Cover and pulse on and off until the mixture starts to swirl evenly. Blend on high for 20 seconds, or until the drink is completely smooth.

 Variations

BANANA BERRY SMOOTHIE Add 2 bananas, peeled and broken into pieces, before blending.

COCONUT BERRY SMOOTHIE Increase the grenadine syrup to 3 tablespoons and add 1/2 cup unsweetened coconut milk before blending.

CULTURED BERRY SMOOTHIE Add 1 cup vanilla yogurt (regular, low-fat, or non-fat) before blending.

ORANGE BERRY SMOOTHIE Add 1 cup orange sherbet before blending.

PEACH BERRY SMOOTHIE Add 1 cup peach sorbet before blending.

PINK BERRY SMOOTHIE Add 1 cup vanilla ice cream before blending.

FUZZY BERRY COCKTAIL Reduce the cranberry juice to ¼ cup. Add 2 ounces vodka and 2 ounces peach schnapps before blending.

VERY BERRY COCKTAIL Reduce the cranberry juice to ¼ cup. Add 4 ounces gold rum before blending.

WHITE RUSSIAN WINTER

To soften ice cream, simply let it sit at room temperature for 10 to 15 minutes before using it.

1 cup ice

½ cup coffee ice cream, softened

¼ cup milk

2 ounces coffee liqueur (such as Kahlúa)

1 ounce vodka or coffee vodka

Combine all the ingredients in a blender. Cover and pulse on and off until the mixture starts to swirl evenly. Blend on high for 20 seconds, or until the drink is completely smooth.

Variations

DARK RUSSIAN FALL Omit the coffee ice cream and coffee liqueur. Add ½ cup chocolate ice cream, 1 ounce dark crème de cacao, and 1 ounce cinnamon schnapps before blending.

PINK RUSSIAN SPRING Omit the coffee ice cream and coffee liqueur. Add ½ cup strawberry ice cream and 2 ounces raspberry liqueur (such as Chambord or crème de framboise) before blending.

YELLOW RUSSIAN SUMMER Omit the coffee ice cream and coffee liqueur. Add ½ cup peach ice cream and 2 ounces peach schnapps before blending.

YELLOW BIRD FREEZE

For a thicker drink, I use frozen pineapple. Simply drain canned pineapple chunks, measure them, then freeze them in a single layer on a plate or cookie sheet. I do this ahead of time and store them in plastic bags in the freezer.

1 cup ice

½ cup canned pineapple chunks, drained and frozen

½ cup pineapple juice

½ cup vanilla ice cream

1 ounce gold rum

1½ ounces coffee liqueur (such as Kahlúa)

Combine all the ingredients in a blender. Cover and pulse on and off until the mixture starts to swirl evenly. Blend on high for 20 seconds, or until the drink is completely smooth.

Variations

BLUE JAY FREEZE Omit the coffee liqueur. Add 1½ ounces blue curaçao before blending.

DOUBLE YELLOW BIRD FREEZE Omit the coffee liqueur. Add 1½ ounces crème de banane before blending.

GREEN PARROT FREEZE Omit the coffee liqueur. Add 1½ ounces melon liqueur (such as Midori) before blending.

PURPLE HUMMINGBIRD FREEZE Omit the coffee liqueur. Add 1½ ounces Parfait Amour before blending.

RED BIRD FREEZE Omit the coffee liqueur. Add 1½ ounces crème de cassis before blending.

Zero-Proof Variation

MELLOW YELLOW BIRD FREEZE Omit the rum and coffee liqueur. Add ¼ cup coffee syrup before blending.

UP OR ON THE ROCKS

EVERYDAY FAVORITES,

SOPHISTICATED HIGHBALLS,

AND OUTRAGEOUS

THIRST QUENCHERS

B-52 BOMBER

If your party needs a B_{12} booster, mix together these ingredients and offer them as shots. Shaken with ice and served on the rocks, they'll keep your party fueled for hours.

> 1 ounce coffee liqueur (such as Kahlúa)
>
> 1 ounce Irish cream liqueur (such as Baileys)
>
> 1 ounce Grand Marnier

Fill a cocktail shaker three-quarters full with ice. Add all three ingredients, cover, and shake well. Strain into a small cocktail glass with fresh ice. Or you can mix all three ingredients without ice and serve in shot glasses.

Variations

B-53 Add 1 ounce unsweetened coconut milk before shaking.

B-54 Add 1 ounce raspberry liqueur (such as Chambord or crème de framboise) before shaking.

B-55 Add 1 ounce hazelnut liqueur (such as Frangelico) before shaking.

B-56 Add 1 ounce dark crème de cacao before shaking.

B-57 Add 1 ounce white crème de menthe before shaking.

BANGKOK BUZZ

The first time I served this drink was for a group of friends who came over to share Chinese take-out. They couldn't believe how delicious it was, and I couldn't believe how simple it was to make. In fact, with only two ingredients, it was easier than ordering in dinner. If your local gourmet store doesn't carry lychee juice simply call Central Market (800-360-2552) or Healthy Pleasures Village (212-353-3663), and it'll show up at your door!

> 1½ ounces coconut rum (such as Malibu)
> 4 ounces lychee juice (see above)

Fill a cocktail shaker three-quarters full with ice. Add both ingredients, cover, and shake well. Strain into a small cocktail glass with fresh ice.

Variations

BANANA BANGKOK BUZZ Add ½ ounce crème de banane before shaking.

CHERRY BANGKOK BUZZ Add ½ ounce cherry liqueur (such as Heering) before shaking.

GINGER BANGKOK BUZZ Add ½ ounce ginger liqueur (such as the Original Canton) before shaking.

MANGO BANGKOK BUZZ Add 1 ounce (2 tablespoons) mango nectar before shaking.

THAI ONE ON Add ½ ounce ginger liqueur, ½ ounce cherry liqueur, ½ ounce crème de banane, and 1 ounce mango nectar before shaking. Makes 2 drinks.

BLOODY MARY AND THE BLOODY DOZEN

It's not your grandfather's Bloody Mary anymore.

> 2 ounces vodka
>
> 4 ounces tomato juice
>
> 1/2 ounce lemon juice (1 tablespoon)
>
> 1/2 teaspoon bottled horseradish
>
> 1/4 teaspoon hot pepper sauce
>
> 1/4 teaspoon Worcestershire sauce

Fill a cocktail shaker three-quarters full with ice. Add all the ingredients, cover, and shake well. Strain into a highball glass filled with fresh ice.

Variations

BLOODY CHINA Reduce the vodka to 1½ ounces. Add ½ ounce ginger liqueur (such as the Original Canton) and ⅛ teaspoon Chinese five-spice powder before shaking.

BLOODY ENGLISH Omit the vodka and horseradish. Add 2 ounces gin and ½ teaspoon grainy mustard before shaking.

BLOODY MARIA Omit the vodka and lemon juice. Add 2 ounces white tequila, 1 ounce lime juice, and a pinch of cumin before shaking.

BLOODY SLUSH Combine all the ingredients except for the vodka, and pour into an ice-cube tray. Freeze until solid. Add the tomato ice cubes to a blender with the vodka. Cover and pulse the blender on and off until the drink is slushy.

BLOODY TROPICS Omit the vodka. Add 2 ounces dark rum before shaking.

BLOODY CLAM Omit the vodka. Add 2 ounces clam juice before shaking.

BLOODY RABBIT Omit the vodka. Add 2 ounces carrot juice, ½ teaspoon chopped fresh dill, and ¼ teaspoon celery seed before shaking.

BLOODY RANGOON Omit the vodka. Proceed with the recipe as directed. Top the drink with 2 ounces ginger ale.

VIRGIN MARY Simply omit the vodka.

Other Bloody Cocktails

These recipes are not variations and do not use the same ingredients as the Bloody Mary above.

BLOODY BREW Combine equal parts tomato juice and ice-cold beer in a chilled, tall glass.

BLOODY BUBBLY Combine equal parts tomato juice and champagne in a chilled wineglass.

BLOODY CUP #1 Pour 2 ounces Pimm's Cup #1 over ice in a tall glass. Add 4 ounces tomato juice and top with tonic water. Stir gently and serve with a tall cucumber spear.

BLUE LIPS

Don't be fooled by its beautiful blue color—blue curaçao is potently *orange* in flavor.

  2 ounces blue curaçao

  2 ounces white rum

  4 ounces lemonade

Fill a cocktail shaker three-quarters full with ice. Add all three ingredients, cover, and shake well. Strain into chilled martini glasses without ice. Or strain into small cocktail glasses with fresh ice.

Variations

ANOTHER SHADE OF BLUE LIPS Omit the white rum. Add 2 ounces spiced rum (such as Captain Morgan) before shaking.

GREEN LIPS Omit the lemonade. Add 4 ounces pineapple juice before shaking.

PURPLE LIPS Add 1 tablespoon grenadine syrup before shaking.

RED LIPS Omit the blue curaçao. Add 2 ounces crème de noya before shaking.

WHITE LIPS Omit the blue curaçao. Add 2 ounces triple sec before shaking.

BRANDY ALEXANDER UP

MAKES 1 DRINK

A Brandy Alexander has been a welcome party guest since the twenties. This chocolate/brandy concoction is sometimes served up in a chilled martini glass, or sometimes on the rocks. You can also try its frozen cousin on page 23.

  1 ounce brandy

  1 ounce dark crème de cacao

  1 ounce heavy cream (2 tablespoons)

Fill a cocktail shaker three-quarters full with ice. Add all the ingredients, cover, and shake well. Strain into a chilled martini glass without ice. Or strain into a small cocktail glass with fresh ice.

Variations

APRICOT ALEXANDER Reduce the crème de cacao to ½ ounce. Add ½ ounce apricot liqueur (such as Apry) before shaking.

BUTTERED-UP ALEXANDER Reduce the crème de cacao to ½ ounce. Add ½ ounce butterscotch schnapps before shaking.

COFFEE ALEXANDER Reduce the crème de cacao to ½ ounce. Add ½ ounce coffee liqueur (such as Kahlúa) before shaking.

GINGER ALEXANDER Reduce the crème de cacao to ½ ounce. Add ½ ounce ginger liqueur (such as the Original Canton) before shaking.

RASPBERRY ALEXANDER Reduce the crème de cacao to ½ ounce. Add ½ ounce raspberry liqueur (such as Chambord or crème de framboise) before shaking.

ROOTIN' TOOTIN' ALEXANDER Reduce the crème de cacao to ½ ounce. Add ½ ounce root beer schnapps before shaking.

CAIPIRINHA

Made from cachaça, a Brazilian rum, this drink is fun to make and is always a hit. It can be made one at a time, but if you are having a large crowd over, make this South American favorite punch-style (page 137).

1 lime, washed

2 teaspoons superfine sugar

2 ounces cachaça

Cut the lime into eighths and place the pieces in a small tumbler. Add the sugar. Using the handle of a wooden spoon, crush the lime wedges. Continue to muddle the mixture until the sugar is dissolved. Fill the glass with crushed ice, or very small ice cubes, and top with cachaça. Stir gently.

Variations

FRENCH CAIPIRINHA   Reduce the cachaça to 1½ ounces. Add ½ ounce crème de cassis with the cachaça.

GRAND CAIPIRINHA   Reduce the cachaça to 1½ ounces. Add ½ ounce Grand Marnier with the cachaça.

JAMAICAN CAIPIRINHA   Reduce the cachaça to 1½ ounces. Add ½ ounce coconut rum (such as Malibu) with the cachaça.

JUNGLE CAIPIRINHA   Reduce the cachaça to 1½ ounces. Add ½ ounce crème de banane with the cachaça.

PORTUGUESE CAIPIRINHA   Reduce the cachaça to 1½ ounces. Add ½ ounce Madeira wine with the cachaça.

CHAMPAGNE COCKTAIL CLASSIC

Some people say you should never use good champagne in a champagne cocktail. They say you'll never taste it. I say use the best champagne you can comfortably afford. Despite the addition of juice, sugar, or other flavoring, your guests will notice the tight, tiny bubbles and yeasty aroma of fine champagne.

 1 sugar cube
 3 dashes bitters
 ½ ounce brandy
 Champagne

Place the sugar cube in the bottom of a champagne flute. Add the bitters to soak into the sugar cube. Add the brandy and fill the glass with champagne.

Other Champagne Cocktails

These recipes are not variations and do not use the same ingredients as the Champagne Cocktail Classic.

BELLINI Fill a champagne flute one-quarter full with peach nectar. Add ½ ounce peach schnapps. Top with champagne.

CHAMPAGNE RICKY Add 1 small scoop lime sherbet to a white wineglass. Top with champagne.

KIR ROYALE Add 1 ounce crème de cassis to a champagne flute. Fill the glass with champagne.

MIMOSA Fill a champagne flute one-third full with orange juice. Top with champagne.

CHAMPAGNE JELL-O SHOTS

These are easy to make, fun, and (dare I say it) an elegant version of the classic college party "drink."

  1 package white grape sparkling Jell-O mix (3 ounces)

  1 cup boiling water

  1 cup chilled champagne

Place the Jell-O in a large mixing bowl and add the boiling water. Stir 2 minutes or until the powder is completely dissolved. Allow the mixture to cool to room temperature. Add the champagne slowly—the mixture will foam. Pour the mixture into an ice-cube tray and let set in the refrigerator for at least 4 hours.

When the Jell-O shots are firm, dip the trays in hot water for 5 seconds to loosen the Jell-O cubes. Run a thin knife around the edges of each cube, then invert over a large bowl to catch the cubes.

Keep refrigerated until ready to serve. Serve in small plastic cups or place all the cubes in a chilled punch bowl and let your guests serve themselves with ice tongs.

Variations

CHERRY BRANDY JELL-O SHOTS Follow the same technique using cherry Jell-O and brandy.

LEMON VODKA JELL-O SHOTS Follow the same technique using lemon Jell-O and vodka or lemon vodka.

ORANGE GIN JELL-O SHOTS Follow the same technique using orange Jell-O and gin.

PINEAPPLE RUM JELL-O SHOTS Follow the same technique using pineapple Jell-O and white rum.

RASPBERRY WHISKEY JELL-O SHOTS Follow the same technique using raspberry Jell-O and blended whiskey.

TEQUILA LIME JELL-O SHOTS Follow the same technique using lime Jell-O and tequila.

CHI-CHI

MAKES 2 DRINKS

I like to think of this as a Piña Colada from Moscow.

3 ounces vodka

3 tablespoons sweetened cream of coconut

1/2 cup pineapple juice

Fill a cocktail shaker three-quarters full with ice. Add all three ingredients, cover, and shake well. Strain into cocktail glasses with fresh ice.

Variations

APRICOT CHI-CHI Reduce the pineapple juice to 1/4 cup. Add 1/4 cup apricot nectar before shaking.

BANANA CHI-CHI Reduce the cream of coconut to 2 tablespoons. Add 1/2 ounce crème de banane before shaking.

CHERRY CHI-CHI Reduce the cream of coconut to 2 tablespoons. Add 1/2 ounce cherry liqueur (such as Heering) before shaking.

LOUISIANA CHI-CHI Add 2 to 3 dashes Tabasco sauce (or more to taste) before shaking.

PEACHY CHI-CHI Reduce the cream of coconut to 2 tablespoons. Add 1/2 ounce peach schnapps before shaking.

SOUTH SEAS CHI-CHI Omit the pineapple juice. Add 1/2 cup passion fruit juice before shaking.

SPICY NUTTY CHI-CHI Reduce the cream of coconut to 2 tablespoons. Add 1 tablespoon hazelnut liqueur (such as Frangelico) and a pinch of ground mace before shaking.

COSMOPOLITAN

MAKES 1 DRINK

There's not a party in town where you won't find these. Some people like theirs sweeter—that's why the sugar is optional.

2 ounces vodka

1 ounce Cointreau

1 ounce cranberry juice cocktail

Juice of 1/2 lime

1/2 teaspoon superfine sugar (optional)

Fill a cocktail shaker three-quarters full with ice. Add all the ingredients, cover, and shake well. Strain into a chilled martini glass without ice. Or strain into a small cocktail glass with fresh ice.

Variations

COSMOPOLITAN COWBOY Use pepper vodka instead of plain vodka.

COSMOPOLITAN MORNING Use coffee vodka instead of plain vodka.

METROPOLITAN Use currant vodka instead of plain vodka.

SERVING SUGGESTION: Before filling your glass, run the cut lime around the rim of the glass, then invert the glass onto a plate of granulated sugar. This will leave a sugar rim, adding a touch of sweetness to the drink. If you serve any of these drinks this way, you should omit the sugar from the recipe.

CRANBERRY SEA BREEZE

This refreshing, classic cocktail is perfect for any party. It can also be made into a punch by multiplying the ingredients by the number of people you're having over. Simply mix everything together over ice in a large pitcher or punch bowl. If you're making one of the variations, garnish the pitcher or bowl with lots of fruit to match the flavor you've chosen.

1 1/2 ounces vodka

2 ounces cranberry juice cocktail

2 ounces grapefruit juice

Fill an iced tea glass three-quarters full with ice. Add all the ingredients and stir gently.

Variations

BLACKBERRY BREEZE   Add 1/2 ounce blackberry liqueur before stirring.

CALIFORNIA BREEZE   Omit the grapefruit juice. Add 2 ounces orange juice and 1/2 ounce triple sec before stirring.

CANDY APPLE BREEZE   Add 1/2 ounce apple schnapps and 1/2 teaspoon grenadine syrup before stirring.

COCONUT BREEZE   Add 1/2 ounce coconut rum (such as Malibu) before stirring.

MONKEY BREEZE   Add 1/2 ounce crème de banane before stirring.

DAIQUIRI . . . UP

Along with the martini, the daiquiri is a classic party drink. Although most people think of daiquiris as frozen and fruity, it all started *up*. If you really miss the ice, go ahead and serve these on the rocks. After all, it's your party.

    3 ounces white rum
    Juice of 1 lime
    1 teaspoon superfine sugar

Fill a cocktail shaker three-quarters full with ice. Add all three ingredients, cover, and shake well. Strain into chilled martini glasses without ice. Or strain into small cocktail glasses with fresh ice.

Variations

ALMOND DAIQUIRI Add ½ ounce almond liqueur (such as crème de noya or amaretto) before shaking.

APPLE DAIQUIRI Add ½ ounce apple schnapps before shaking.

APRICOT DAIQUIRI Add ½ ounce apricot brandy or apricot liqueur (such as Apry) before shaking.

BLACKBERRY DAIQUIRI Add ½ ounce blackberry liqueur before shaking.

BLACK CURRANT DAIQUIRI Add ½ ounce crème de cassis before shaking.

BLUE AND ORANGE DAIQUIRI Add ½ ounce blue curaçao before shaking.

CHERRY DAIQUIRI Add ½ ounce cherry liqueur (such as Heering) before shaking.

GINGER DAIQUIRI Add ½ ounce ginger liqueur (such as the Original Canton) before shaking.

GREEN MELON DAIQUIRI Add ½ ounce melon liqueur (such as Midori) before shaking.

HONEY DAIQUIRI Add ½ ounce honey liqueur (such as Bärenjäger) before shaking.

PURPLE PASSION DAIQUIRI Add ½ ounce Parfait Amour before shaking.

RASPBERRY DAIQUIRI Add ½ ounce raspberry liqueur (such as Chambord or crème de framboise) before shaking.

DIM SUM SLING

Ginger liqueur gives this drink an unmistakable Asian flavor—delicate, understated, and smooth.

    1 ounce vodka

    1/2 ounce ginger liqueur (such as the Original Canton)

    1/2 ounce pear liqueur

    3 ounces pear nectar

Fill a cocktail shaker three-quarters full with ice. Add all the ingredients, cover, and shake well. Strain into a cocktail glass with fresh ice.

Variations

CALIFORNIA DIM SUM SLING Omit the pear nectar. Add 3 ounces white grape juice before shaking.

HAWAIIAN DIM SUM SLING Omit the pear nectar. Add 3 ounces pineapple juice before shaking.

MASSACHUSETTS DIM SUM SLING Omit the pear nectar. Add 3 ounces cranberry juice cocktail before shaking.

WASHINGTON DIM SUM SLING Omit the pear nectar. Add 3 ounces apple cider before shaking.

WISCONSIN DIM SUM SLING Omit the pear nectar. Add 3 ounces cherry juice before shaking.

FRAT BOYS DO LUNCH

It's a long walk to the nearest keg party.

2 ounces gin

1 ounce cherry liqueur (such as Heering)

3 ounces lemonade

2 ounces passion fruit juice

Fill a cocktail shaker three-quarters full with ice. Add all the ingredients, cover, and shake well. Strain into a highball glass with fresh ice.

Variations

FRAT BOYS DO BREAKFAST Omit the lemonade. Add 3 ounces orange juice before shaking.

FRAT BOYS DO BRUNCH Omit the lemonade. Add 3 ounces tomato juice before shaking and top with 1 or 2 shakes of hot pepper sauce.

FRAT BOYS DO DINNER Omit the lemonade. Add 3 ounces cranberry juice cocktail before shaking.

FRAT BOYS DO PICNICS Omit the lemonade. Add 3 ounces apple juice before shaking.

FRAT BOYS DO TEA Omit the lemonade. Add 3 ounces sweetened iced tea before shaking.

GIN AND COCONUT WATER

Thanks, Jimmy Buffett! If it weren't for his lyrics, this drink would never have crossed my lips. Coconut water is the liquid found inside young, unripe coconuts. Coconut water is also available in cans in many supermarkets and most Latin markets or by mail from Central Market (800-360-2552).

> 4 ounces gin
>
> 6 ounces coconut water

Fill a cocktail shaker three-quarters full with ice. Add both ingredients, cover, and shake well. Strain into small cocktail glasses with fresh ice.

Variations

COCONUT GIMLET Add 1 ounce sweetened bottled lime juice before shaking.

ORANGE GIN AND COCONUTS Add 2 teaspoons orange flower water before shaking.

PASSION COCONUT PUNCH Reduce the coconut water to 4 ounces. Add 2 ounces passion fruit juice before shaking.

PINK ISLAND GIN Add ½ ounce grenadine syrup before shaking.

ROSY GIN AND COCONUTS Add 1 teaspoon rose water before shaking.

GUANABANANA

Although guanabana fruit is not often available in American markets, guanabana nectar or juice is available almost everywhere. It's delicately floral, creamy white, incredibly delicious. And it blends perfectly with bananas.

  1 ounce white rum

  1 ounce crème de banane

  1/2 ounce cherry liqueur (such as Heering)

  3 ounces guanabana nectar

  1 1/2 ounces banana nectar

Fill a cocktail shaker three-quarters full with ice. Add all the ingredients, cover, and shake well. Strain into a highball glass with fresh ice.

Variations

CHOCOLATE GUANABANANA Omit the cherry liqueur. Add 1/2 ounce white crème de cocoa before shaking.

COCONUT GUANABANANA Omit the white rum. Add 1 ounce coconut rum (such as Malibu) before shaking.

ORANGE GUANABANANA Omit the cherry liqueur. Add 1/2 ounce triple sec before shaking.

RASPBERRY GUANABANANA Omit the cherry liqueur. Add 1/2 ounce raspberry liqueur (such as Chambord or crème de framboise) before shaking.

 ## Zero-Proof Variation

VIRGIN GUANABANANA Follow the same technique using 1/2 cup guanabana nectar, 1/4 cup banana nectar, 2 tablespoons grenadine syrup, and the juice of 1 lime.

HURRICANE (CATEGORY 1)

Weathermen list hurricanes by category—the higher the number, the more potent the storm. This is also a fun way to let your guests know what kind of *Hurricane* you're serving.

1 ounce white rum

½ ounce dark rum

2 ounces passion fruit juice

2 ounces lemonade

1 ounce orange juice

Juice of ½ lime

½ teaspoon grenadine syrup

Fill a cocktail shaker three-quarters full with ice. Add all the ingredients, cover, and shake well. Strain into a highball glass or hurricane glass with fresh ice.

Variations

HURRICANE (CATEGORY 2) Increase the white rum to 1½ ounces.

HURRICANE (CATEGORY 3) Increase the white rum to 1½ ounces and add ½ ounce crème de banane before shaking.

HURRICANE (CATEGORY 4) Increase the white rum to 1½ ounces, add ½ ounce crème de banane and ½ ounce peach schnapps before shaking.

HURRICANE (CATEGORY 5) Increase the white rum to 1½ ounces, increase the dark rum to 1 ounce, and add ½ ounce crème de banane and ½ ounce peach schnapps before shaking.

JADE

The flavor of this gem is sweet and tart. The variations have beautiful colors, so you can make them to match what your guests are wearing.

1 1/2 ounces white rum

1/2 ounce triple sec

Juice of 1/2 lime

1 teaspoon powdered sugar

1/2 teaspoon green crème de menthe

Fill a cocktail shaker three-quarters full with ice. Add all the ingredients, cover, and shake well. Strain into a chilled martini glass.

Variations

AMETHYST Omit the triple sec and green crème de menthe. Add 1/2 ounce Parfait Amour and 1/2 teaspoon white crème de menthe before shaking.

GARNET Omit the triple sec and green crème de menthe. Add 1/2 ounce red curaçao and 1/2 teaspoon white crème de menthe before shaking.

OPAL Omit the triple sec and green crème de menthe. Add 1/2 ounce Cointreau and 1/2 teaspoon white crème de menthe before shaking.

TOPAZ Omit the triple sec and green crème de menthe. Add 1/2 ounce Grand Marnier and 1/2 teaspoon white crème de menthe before shaking.

TURQUOISE Omit the triple sec and green crème de menthe. Add 1/2 ounce blue curaçao and 1/2 teaspoon white crème de menthe before shaking.

LONG ISLAND ICED TEA

This party powerhouse is made at every beach bash and summer fling from Montauk to Montego Bay. Be forewarned: They are stronger than they taste.

1 ounce vodka

1 ounce gin

1 ounce white rum

1 ounce white tequila

1 ounce triple sec

1 ounce lemon juice

Cola

Two lemon wedges for garnish

Fill a cocktail shaker three-quarters full with ice. Add all the ingredients except the cola and lemon wedges, cover, and shake well. Strain into iced tea glasses with fresh ice. Top with enough cola to fill the glasses. Garnish each glass with a wedge of lemon.

Variations

MASON-DIXON ICED TEA Omit the triple sec. Add 1 ounce Southern Comfort before shaking.

SHANGHAI ICED TEA Omit the triple sec. Add 1 ounce ginger liqueur (such as the Original Canton) before shaking.

TOKYO ICED TEA Omit the tequila. Add 1 ounce sake before shaking.

VERSAILLES ICED TEA Omit the triple sec. Add 1 ounce raspberry liqueur (such as Chambord or crème de framboise) before shaking.

LYNCHBURG LEMONADE

Proof positive that Southerners do know how to have a helluva good time. One trick I learned down in Texas is to mix enough of this up before company comes and simply shake each drink with ice as the glasses empty out. It's fast, it's easy, and it keeps you out of the kitchen.

1 ounce bourbon

1 ounce triple sec

Juice of 1 lemon

1 teaspoon superfine sugar

Lemon-lime soda

Fill a cocktail shaker three-quarters full with ice. Add all the ingredients except the lemon-lime soda, cover, and shake well. Strain into an iced tea glass with fresh ice. Top with enough lemon-lime soda to fill the glass.

Variations

LYNCHBURG GINGER LEMONADE Omit the triple sec. Add 1 ounce ginger liqueur (such as the Original Canton) before shaking. Top with ginger ale instead of lemon-lime soda.

LYNCHBURG LEMONADE PUNCH Multiply all the ingredients by ten and place in a large pitcher filled with ice. Stir well and add 1 liter lemon-lime soda. Makes 10 drinks.

LYNCHBURG PINK LEMONADE Omit the sugar. Add 2 teaspoons grenadine syrup before shaking.

MAI-TAI

This Polynesian classic clamors for paper umbrellas along with a pupu platter.

1½ ounces white rum

1 ounce Grand Marnier

Juice of ½ lime

2 teaspoons almond syrup

1 teaspoon powdered sugar

1 teaspoon grenadine syrup (optional)

Fill a cocktail shaker three-quarters full with ice. Add all the ingredients, cover, and shake well. Strain into a cocktail glass with fresh ice.

Variations

APRICOT MAI-TAI Omit the Grand Marnier. Add 1 ounce apricot brandy before shaking.

AUNT BEE'S MAI-TAI Omit the grenadine syrup. Add ½ ounce honey liqueur (such as Bärenjäger) before shaking.

CHERRY TREE MAI-TAI Omit the grenadine syrup. Add ½ ounce cherry liqueur (such as Heering) before shaking.

GOLDEN MAI-TAI Omit the grenadine syrup. Add ½ ounce cinnamon schnapps (such as Goldschläger) before shaking.

MONKEY MAI-TAI Omit the grenadine syrup. Add ½ ounce crème de banane before shaking.

PEACHY MAI-TAI Omit the Grand Marnier. Add 1 ounce peach schnapps before shaking.

MANHATTAN

Perfect for a party on Park Avenue or Main Street.

1½ ounces blended whiskey
¼ ounce sweet red vermouth
¼ ounce dry white vermouth

Fill a cocktail shaker three-quarters full with ice. Add all the ingredients, cover, and shake well. Strain into a small cocktail glass filled with fresh ice.

Variations

DRY MANHATTAN Omit the sweet vermouth and increase the dry vermouth to ½ ounce. Garnish with a lemon twist.

LATIN MANHATTAN Omit the whiskey. Add 1½ ounces gold rum before shaking. Garnish with a pineapple spear.

SWEET MANHATTAN Omit the dry vermouth and increase the sweet vermouth to ½ ounce. Garnish with 1 or 2 maraschino cherries.

MAPLE BREW-HAHA

Maple-*flavored* syrup might be perfectly fine for pancakes and French toast, but I want only 100 percent pure maple syrup in my cocktails.

   1½ ounces coffee liqueur (such as Kahlúa)

   ½ ounce vodka

   3 ounces whole milk

   ½ ounce pure maple syrup

   Pinch ground cinnamon

Fill a cocktail shaker three-quarters full with ice. Add all the ingredients, cover, and shake well. Strain into a cocktail glass with fresh ice.

Variations

ALMOND MAPLE BREW Omit the cinnamon. Add 1 teaspoon almond-flavored syrup before shaking.

BANANA MAPLE BREW Substitute banana nectar for the milk. This drink is dairy-free!

CHERRY MAPLE BREW Omit the cinnamon. Add 1 tablespoon cherry syrup before shaking.

CHOCOHOLIC'S MAPLE BREW Add 1 tablespoon chocolate syrup before shaking.

HAZELNUT MAPLE BREW Omit the cinnamon. Add 1 teaspoon hazelnut syrup before shaking.

MARGARITA

The margarita is one of the most ordered bar drinks of all time, yet there are as many ways to make one as there are bartenders making them. I like this formula because it not only tastes great, but the liquid ingredients are all equal parts, so I can multiply the recipe for a crowd without utilizing higher math.

> 1 ounce white tequila
>
> 1 ounce triple sec
>
> 1 ounce fresh lime juice
>
> 1 teaspoon superfine sugar

Fill a cocktail shaker three-quarters full with ice. Add all the ingredients, cover, and shake well. Strain into a small cocktail glass with fresh ice.

SERVING SUGGESTION: Before making the drink, wet the edge of the glass with lime juice, then dip it in coarse salt. Fill with ice and prepare the drink.

Variations

BLACKBERRY MARGARITA Omit the sugar. Add 1 ounce blackberry liqueur before shaking.

BLUE MARGARITA Omit the triple sec. Add 1 ounce blue curaçao before shaking.

HONEY MARGARITA Omit the sugar. Add 1 ounce honey liqueur (such as Bärenjäger) before shaking.

PEACHY MARGARITA Omit the sugar. Add 1 ounce peach schnapps before shaking.

RASPBERRY MARGARITA Omit the sugar. Add 1 ounce raspberry liqueur (such as Chambord or crème de framboise) before shaking.

TOP SHELF MARGARITA Omit the white tequila and triple sec. Add 1 ounce premium tequila (such as Jose Cuervo Tradicional or Sauza Conmemorativo) and 1 ounce Cointreau before shaking.

MARTINI—DRY

The controversy over martinis is endless. The purists among us insist that a martini is gin and vermouth, garnished with an olive or two. End of discussion. Although that is where the martini started, it's changed over the years. First, vinegar from the olive jar was added and a dirty martini was born. Next, cocktail onions replaced olives, and a Gibson was served. Soon, vodka replaced the gin, and we had a vodka martini. Today, as chefs battle it out on TV to come up with the most unusual dishes they can, so bartenders try to see who can create the most unusual "martini." It seems the only requirement is that the drink be served in a chilled martini glass. So let's start at the very beginning—the classic dry martini—and take it from there.

1 1/2 ounces gin

1 1/2 teaspoons dry vermouth

1 or 2 two olives for garnish (see note below)

Fill a martini glass with ice and let sit while you prepare the drink.

Fill a shaker or tall glass half full with ice. Add the gin and vermouth. Stir gently with a long thin swizzle stick or even a skewer. You don't want to break up the ice, simply have it chill the drink well. Empty the ice out of the prepared martini glass, and strain the drink into it. Garnish with an olive or two.

Note: Martini olives are pitted, often stuffed with pimientos, and usually marinated in vermouth. They are available in almost every supermarket.

Variations

BALSAMIC MARTINI Add 1 teaspoon aged balsamic vinegar along with the vermouth. This drink only works with aged balsamic vinegar, a sweet, syrupy (and expensive) vinegar available in gourmet shops or by mail from Central Market (800-360-2552).

BERRY BERRY MARTINI Omit the gin and vermouth. Add 2 ounces currant vodka and 2 teaspoons raspberry liqueur (such as Chambord or crème de framboise). Proceed with the recipe as directed. Garnish with fresh berries.

BITTERINI Omit the gin and vermouth. Add 2 ounces orange vodka and ¾ ounce Campari. Proceed with the recipe as directed. Garnish with lemon twist.

BLUE MOON MARTINI Omit the gin and vermouth. Add 2 ounces Bombay Sapphire gin, 2 teaspoons dry vermouth, and 1 teaspoon blue curaçao. Proceed with the recipe as directed. Garnish with an orange wheel.

CONFEDERATE MARTINI Omit the vermouth. Add ½ ounce Southern Comfort. Proceed with the recipe as directed. Garnish with a dried peach.

EXTRA-DRY MARTINI Do not add the vermouth to the ice along with the gin. Instead, add the vermouth to the chilled martini glass. Swirl it around and discard before adding the chilled gin.

EXTRA-EXTRA-DRY MARTINI Omit the vermouth entirely. (Simply wave the bottle over the chilled gin before serving.)

LEMONTINI Omit the vermouth. Add ½ ounce lemon liqueur (such as Limoncello). Proceed with the recipe as directed. Garnish with a lemon twist.

MINTINI Omit the vermouth. Add 1½ teaspoons green crème de menthe. Proceed with the recipe as directed. Garnish with fresh mint leaves.

SAKETINI Omit the gin. Add 2 ounces dry sake. Proceed with recipe as directed. Garnish with pickled ginger.

SWEET AND SPICY MARTINI Omit the gin and vermouth. Add 2 ounces pepper vodka and ½ ounce sweet red vermouth. Proceed with the recipe as directed. Garnish with black peppercorns.

SWEET FRENCH MARTINI Omit the gin and vermouth. Add 1½ ounces vodka and 1½ ounces white Lillet wine. Proceed with the recipe as directed. Garnish with an orange twist.

SWEET MARTINI Add up to ¾ ounce (1½ tablespoons) vermouth.

TEQUINI Omit the gin. Add 2 ounces white tequila. Proceed with the recipe as directed. Garnish with pickled jalapeño.

WHITE CHOCOLATE MARTINI Omit the gin and vermouth. Add 2 ounces vodka and 1½ ounces white crème de cacao. Garnish with white chocolate kisses.

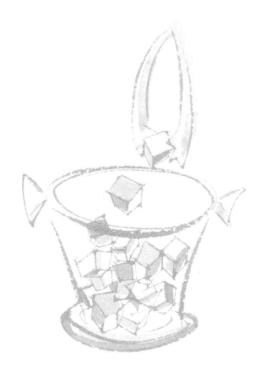

MINT JULEP

An old Southern myth, as told by William Alexander Percy in *Lanterns on the Levee*, says that when you add the bourbon to this drink, it must be stirred by a beautiful woman.

12 fresh mint leaves

2 teaspoons sugar

2 teaspoons water

2½ ounces bourbon

Place 8 mint leaves in the bottom of a highball glass. Add the sugar and water. Using the back end of a wooden spoon, mash them together until the sugar is dissolved and the mint is "bruised." Fill the glass with crushed ice, and slide the remaining mint leaves halfway down the sides of the glass. Add the bourbon. Sip slowly for hours.

Variations

BASIL JULEP Use fresh basil leaves instead of mint leaves.

TARRAGON JULEP Use fresh tarragon leaves instead of mint leaves.

PEACH WINE COOLER

You may never serve another wine spritzer again!

4 ounces dry white wine (such as Chablis)

1 ounce peach schnapps

2 ounces orange juice

2 ounces pineapple juice

Fill a cocktail shaker three-quarters full with ice. Add all the ingredients, cover, and shake well. Strain into a wineglass with fresh ice.

Variations

CHERRY PEACH WINE COOLER Add 1 ounce cherry syrup before shaking.

DOUBLE PEACH WINE COOLER Omit the pineapple juice. Add 2 ounces peach nectar before shaking.

FLORIDA PEACH WINE COOLER Omit the pineapple juice. Add 2 ounces grapefruit juice before shaking.

PARISIAN PEACH WINE COOLER Use white Lillet wine instead of regular white wine. Lillet is a sweetened orange-scented wine from France, and is available at most liquor stores.

PEACHY PLUM WINE COOLER Omit the white wine. Add 4 ounces Japanese plum wine before shaking.

TROPICAL PEACH WINE COOLER Omit the orange juice. Add 2 ounces guava nectar before blending.

PINEAPPLE VODKA SHOOTERS

You must use fresh pineapple for this party starter, and you must plan a week in advance to allow the flavors to meld.

    1 large, ripe pineapple

    1 bottle vodka (750 milliliters)

    ½ vanilla bean, split lengthwise

    2 heaping tablespoons sugar

Cut the rind away from the pineapple and slice the fruit away from the core. Cut the fruit into 1-inch chunks and place them with any accumulated juices into a large covered jar or container. Add the vodka (rinse out and save the bottle), vanilla bean, and sugar. Stir well, then cover and set in a cool, dark place for 1 week. Strain the mixture and discard the vanilla bean. Save the pineapple to enjoy later on. Pour the vodka back into its original bottle and store in the freezer. The vodka will not freeze. Serve in chilled shot glasses. Or serve over ice, topped with ginger ale or orange or cranberry juice.

Variations

CRANBERRY PINEAPPLE VODKA Add 1 cup dried cranberries along with the pineapple.

MULLED PINEAPPLE VODKA Add 2 tablespoons mulling spices along with the vanilla bean.

SPICE-INFUSED VODKA Instead of the pineapple, sugar, and vanilla bean, try adding one of the following: ½ cup fresh sliced ginger, 2 split jalapeño peppers, or 2 cinnamon sticks (4-inch pieces). They all make a great-tasting vodka for mixed drinks or served straight from the freezer as shots.

SZECHWAN PINEAPPLE VODKA Omit the vanilla bean. Add 2 tablespoons Szechwan peppercorns with the pineapple. Proceed with the recipe as directed.

PLANTER'S PUNCH

MAKES 1 DRINK

What's a punch recipe doing here? This classic drink is most often made and served one at a time. Feel free to multiply this recipe to serve a crowd—just add the ingredients to a large pitcher or punch bowl filled with ice (page 1), then stir until very cold.

1 ounce white rum

1 ounce gold rum

1 ounce dark rum

2 ounces sweetened bottled lime juice

1/4 cup pineapple juice

1/4 cup orange juice

Fill a cocktail shaker three-quarters full with ice. Add all the ingredients, cover, and shake well. Strain into a highball glass with fresh ice.

Variations

PLANTER'S CHERRY PUNCH Omit the sweetened bottled lime juice. Add 2 ounces sour cherry syrup before shaking.

PLANTER'S COCONUT PUNCH Omit the white rum. Add 1 ounce coconut rum (such as Malibu) before shaking.

PLANTER'S PEACH PUNCH Omit the gold rum. Add 1 ounce peach schnapps before shaking.

SHAKIN' SHOOTERS

These simple drinks are easy to make—which is good, because they're so tasty, they'll disappear as fast as you can make them.

Technique: Simply mix all the ingredients together over ice. Stir or shake to chill. Strain and serve in very small glasses. Each recipe makes 2 drinks.

ASIAN JET LAG

1½ ounces gold rum

1½ ounces mandarin orange liqueur (such as Mandarin Napoleon) or Grand Marnier

½ ounce ginger liqueur (such as the Original Canton)

BERRY BOMB

2 ounces cherry brandy

1 ounce raspberry liqueur (such as Chambord or crème de framboise)

1 ounce vodka or currant vodka

1 teaspoon grenadine syrup

BLUE LEMON

1 ounce blue curaçao

2 ounces vodka or citrus vodka

1 ounce lemonade

CANCUN MORNING

2 ounces gold tequila

1 ounce triple sec

1 ounce fresh orange juice

MELON BALL

1 ounce vodka

1 ounce melon liqueur (such as Midori)

1½ ounces orange juice

PINK SLAMMER

1 ounce vodka

1 1/2 ounces raspberry liqueur

(such as Chambord or crème

de framboise)

1/2 ounce white crème de

cacao

OLD NAVY

2 ounces dark rum

1 ounce sweetened bottled

lime juice

1 ounce coconut rum (such

as Malibu)

TIRAMISU

1 ounce gold rum

1 ounce coffee liqueur (such as

Kahlúa)

1 ounce advokaat liqueur

1 teaspoon cinnamon schnapps

SUMMER SLALOM

2 ounces vodka

1 ounce white crème de menthe

1 ounce melon liqueur (such as

Midori)

WHITE MONKEY

1 ounce white crème de

cacao

1 ounce crème de banane

1 ounce white rum

1/2 ounce half and half

TROPICAL NUT

1 1/2 ounces vodka

1/2 ounce hazelnut liqueur (such

as Frangelico)

1 1/2 ounces pineapple juice

STRIPED SHOOTERS

These are pretty drinks made with layers of liqueurs and syrups. They can be sipped, layer by layer, or drunk quickly in one shot. Either way, use a narrow liqueur glass (sometimes called a pousse café glass—preferably straight-sided) to help keep the layers from mixing. Follow the technique below to create any of the striped shooters listed.

Technique: Pour the first ingredient directly into the bottom of the glass. Slowly pour the next ingredient over the back of a spoon, just touching the top of the previous ingredient. Continue until all the ingredients are used. To ensure clean layers, make sure you pour the ingredients in the order listed. Each recipe makes 1 drink.

ALL-AMERICAN

1/2 ounce grenadine syrup

1/2 ounce white crème de cacao

1/2 ounce blue curaçao

BENGAL TIGER

1/2 ounce butterscotch schnapps

1/2 ounce dark crème de cacao

1/2 ounce Irish cream liqueur (such
as Baileys)

1/2 ounce ginger liqueur
(such as the Original Canton)

BLACK AND WHITE

3/4 ounce coffee liqueur (such as
Kahlúa)

3/4 ounce anise liqueur (such as
sambuca or Pernod)

3/4 ounce Irish cream liqueur
(such as Baileys)

CHOCOLATE BERRY

¾ ounce crème de cassis

¾ ounce white crème de cacao

¾ ounce brandy

½ ounce half and half

CITY OF LIGHT

½ ounce honey liqueur (such as Bärenjäger)

½ ounce Parfait Amour

½ ounce Irish cream liqueur (such as Baileys)

½ ounce Grand Marnier

COUGH DROP

¾ ounce honey liqueur (such as Bärenjäger)

¾ ounce lemon liqueur (such as Limoncello)

¾ ounce brandy

ELIXIR OF LOVE

½ ounce cherry liqueur (such as Heering)

½ ounce Parfait Amour

½ ounce Cointreau

½ ounce brandy

FUZZY MONK

½ ounce Benedictine

½ ounce peach schnapps

½ ounce hazelnut liqueur (such as Frangelico)

½ ounce half and half

NUTTY MONKEY

¾ ounce dark crème de cacao

¾ ounce crème de banane

¾ ounce almond liqueur (such
as amaretto)

PEPPERMINT PATTY

½ ounce dark crème de
cacao

½ ounce white crème de
menthe

½ ounce brandy

½ ounce heavy cream

RAINBOW FLAG

¼ ounce cherry liqueur (such as
Heering)

¼ ounce crème de banane

¼ ounce Parfait Amour

¼ ounce blue curaçao

¼ ounce melon liqueur (such as
Midori)

¼ ounce Grand Marnier

TRAFFIC LIGHT

½ ounce grenadine syrup

½ ounce crème de banane

½ ounce green crème de
menthe (or melon
liqueur, such as Midori)

TEXAS BAYOU BLAST

Be sure to use white lemonade for a psychedelic green color.

¾ cup lemonade

2 ounces melon liqueur (such as Midori)

3 ounces white tequila

½ teaspoon green crème de menthe

Fill a cocktail shaker three-quarters full with ice. Add all the ingredients, cover, and shake well. Strain into chilled martini glasses and serve up. Or strain into highball glasses with fresh ice.

Variations

BAYOU GROVE Reduce the lemonade to ¼ cup. Add ½ cup orange juice before shaking.

HAWAIIAN BAYOU Omit the lemonade. Add ¾ cup pineapple juice before shaking.

MONTEGO BAY BLAST Omit the tequila. Add 3 ounces white rum before shaking.

TOKYO BLAST Omit the crème de menthe and tequila. Add 3 ounces sake before shaking.

THREE-HOUR TOUR

Just the thing for a short boating party or extended stay on a desert island. Simply lie by the lagoon and hope you never get rescued.

- 1 ounce coconut rum (such as Malibu)
- 1 ounce peach schnapps
- 1 ounce melon liqueur (such as Midori)
- 3 ounces orange juice
- 3 ounces cranberry juice cocktail

Fill a cocktail shaker three-quarters full with ice. Add all the ingredients, cover, and shake well. Strain into highball glasses or coconut shells with fresh ice.

Variations

GINGER'S DELIGHT Omit the melon liqueur and orange juice. Add 1 ounce ginger liqueur (such as the Original Canton) and 3 ounces pineapple juice before shaking.

HOWELL'S HOWLER Omit the melon liqueur. Add 1 ounce Grand Marnier before shaking.

LITTLE BUDDY'S BUDDY Omit the coconut rum. Add 1 ounce white rum before shaking.

MARY ANN'S CHOICE Omit the melon liqueur. Add 1 ounce cherry liqueur (such as Heering) before shaking.

PROFESSOR'S PUNCH Omit the melon liqueur. Add 1 ounce crème de banane before shaking.

SKIPPER'S POISON Omit the coconut rum. Add 1 ounce dark rum before shaking.

TOM COLLINS

You can buy collins mixer in almost every supermarket, but it's often filled with artificial flavors and the taste can vary widely among brands. The only way to get a perfect collins every time is to make it yourself, one glass at a time.

    2 ounces gin
    1 ounce lemon juice
    3 teaspoons superfine sugar
    Club soda as needed

Combine the gin, lemon juice, and sugar in a highball glass. Stir until the sugar is dissolved. Pack the glass to the top with ice and fill with club soda. Stir gently.

Variations

BORIS COLLINS Omit the gin. Add 2 ounces vodka. Proceed with the recipe as directed.

CHITA COLLINS Omit the gin. Add 2 ounces white tequila. Proceed with the recipe as directed.

PATRICK COLLINS Omit the gin. Add 2 ounces whiskey. Proceed with the recipe as directed.

RITA COLLINS Omit the gin. Add 2 ounces white rum. Proceed with the recipe as directed.

VIRGIN ISLAND

MAKES 1 DRINK

Can't throw your party at the beach? These drinks will transport your guests there in one sip.

1/4 cup passion fruit juice

1/4 cup banana nectar

1/4 cup mango nectar

1 teaspoon grenadine syrup

Fill a cocktail shaker three-quarters full with ice. Add all the ingredients, cover, and shake well. Strain into a cocktail glass with fresh ice.

Variations

ST. CROIX Omit the passion fruit juice and grenadine syrup. Add 1/2 cup lemonade and 1 teaspoon sweetened bottled lime juice before shaking.

ST. JOHN Omit the banana nectar and grenadine syrup. Add 1/4 cup pineapple juice and 1 teaspoon blackberry syrup before shaking.

ST. THOMAS Omit the mango nectar and grenadine syrup. Add 1/4 cup cranberry juice cocktail and 1 teaspoon almond syrup before shaking.

VIRGIN GORDA Omit the passion fruit juice, mango nectar, and grenadine syrup. Add 1/4 cup pineapple juice, 1/4 cup tamarind nectar, and 1 teaspoon vanilla syrup before shaking.

Spiked Variation

TORTOLA Add 2 ounces gold rum to any of the above and they'll be anything but virginal.

WHISKEY SOUR

MAKES 1 DRINK

Make sure there's a maraschino cherry or two waiting for your guests when they get to the bottom of their glasses.

2 ounces whiskey

1 ounce lemon juice

1 teaspoon superfine sugar

Maraschino cherries for garnish

Fill a cocktail shaker three-quarters full with ice. Add all the ingredients, cover, and shake well. Strain into a small cocktail glass filled with fresh ice and a maraschino cherry (or two).

Variations

BLACKBERRY SOUR Omit the whiskey. Add 2 ounces blackberry brandy before shaking.

ISLAND SOUR Omit the whiskey. Add 2 ounces gold rum before shaking.

MEXICAN SOUR Omit the whiskey. Add 2 ounces tequila before shaking.

NORMANDY SOUR Omit the whiskey. Add 2 ounces calvados before shaking.

PARISIAN SOUR Omit the whiskey. Add 2 ounces cognac before shaking.

SOUR CHERRY Omit the whiskey. Add 2 ounces cherry brandy before shaking.

SOUR MONK Omit the whiskey. Add 2 ounces Benedictine before shaking.

SOUR NUT Omit the whiskey. Add 2 ounces almond liqueur (such as crème de noya or amaretto) before shaking.

SOUR PEACH Omit the whiskey. Add 2 ounces peach schnapps before shaking.

SOUTHERN SOUR Omit the whiskey. Add 2 ounces bourbon before shaking.

SUNNY APRICOT SOUR Omit the whiskey. Add 2 ounces apricot brandy before shaking.

PUNCHES

PITCHERS, BOWLS, AND FISH TANK FAVORITES

BERRY BERRY PUNCH

This punch is dark, sweet, delicious, and impossible to get out of the carpet if you spill it.

    1 cup black currant juice

    1 cup concord grape juice

    1 cup cranberry juice cocktail

    2 ounces crème de cassis

    2 ounces blackberry brandy

    2 ounces cherry brandy

    2 ounces raspberry liqueur (such as Chambord or crème de framboise)

    2 ounces currant vodka

    Juice of 1 lemon

Combine all the ingredients in a 2-quart pitcher filled with ice. Stir well and serve over ice.

ⓨ Zero-Proof Variation

SPRING BERRY PUNCH Omit the crème de cassis, blackberry brandy, cherry brandy, raspberry liqueur, and currant vodka. Add 1 cup strawberry juice, 1 cup red currant juice, and 1 cup youngberry juice (optional). Makes about 2½ quarts. Youngberry juice and strawberry juice are available at many gourmet stores or by mail from Central Market (800-360-2552).

BOMBAY PUNCH

MAKES 6 CUPS

This punch is so overflowing with sweet fruit flavor, any gin will do. Save the good stuff for martinis (page 114).

6 ounces gin

4 ounces Southern Comfort

2 ounces crème de banane

1 cup passion fruit juice

1 cup banana nectar

¾ cup mango nectar

Fill a large pitcher with ice. Add all the ingredients and stir well.

Variations

BLUE BOMBAY PUNCH Omit the Southern Comfort. Add 4 ounces blue curaçao along with the rest of the ingredients.

DESERT SUN PUNCH Add 1 tablespoon grenadine syrup along with the rest of the ingredients.

CAIPIRINHA PUNCH

I like to make this punch in a large, insulated drink cooler so the ice stays frozen as long as possible. I also make sure my guests get lime wedges and ice in each serving. This recipe makes over a gallon, or enough for up to 24 people. If you want to make less, simply divide the recipe in half, or even in quarters.

24 limes, washed

1 cup superfine sugar

6 quarts crushed ice (page 1) or small ice cubes

1 bottle cachaça (1 liter)

Cut the limes into eighths. Place in a large bowl or cooler, and add the sugar. Crush the limes with a potato masher or a large wooden spoon, and continue to mix until the sugar is dissolved. Add the ice and cachaça and stir.

Variations

CHERRY CAIPIRINHA PUNCH Add one jar maraschino cherries and their syrup, along with the cachaça.

TEXAS-STYLE YUCCA Follow the same technique as for Caipirinha Punch, substituting 24 lemons for the limes, and 1 liter tequila for the cachaça.

YUCCA Follow the same technique as for Caipirinha Punch, substituting 24 lemons for the limes.

CHAMPAGNE PUNCH

You don't have to pit the cherries for this punch, because you're going to strain them out later, but if you'd like to blend them up with ice for a daiquiri or an adult smoothie, you must pit them first.

1 quart sweet cherries (fresh or frozen)

1 bottle kirsh (1 pint)

2 bottles champagne (750 milliliters each)

Crush the cherries lightly with a potato masher or with your hands. Add the kirsh. Cover and refrigerate for at least 2 days. Strain the kirsch through a sieve and discard the cherry pulp and pits.

Place a large block of ice (page 1) in a medium punch bowl. Add the kirsh, pour in the champagne, and stir.

Variations

ARABIAN CHAMPAGNE PUNCH Omit the cherries. Add 1 quart fresh, crushed figs to the kirsch.

FUZZY CHAMPAGNE PUNCH Omit the cherries. Add 2 cups sliced, pitted peaches and 2 cups sliced, pitted apricots to the kirsch.

SUMMER CHAMPAGNE PUNCH Omit the cherries. Add 2 cups sliced, pitted plums and 2 cups sliced, pitted nectarines to the kirsch.

TROPICAL CHAMPAGNE PUNCH Omit the cherries. Add 2 cups peeled, chopped papaya and 2 cups peeled, chopped mango to the kirsch.

EGGNOG

For safety, these eggs are cooked. This also makes a richer, creamier, more decadent drink.

    1 cup sugar

    12 egg yolks

    4 cups whole milk

    1 cup heavy cream

    8 ounces brandy

    4 ounces gold rum

    1 tablespoon vanilla extract

    1/2 teaspoon ground nutmeg

Beat the sugar into the egg yolks until thickened and pale yellow. Set aside.

Bring the milk to a simmer in a large saucepan over medium heat. Slowly beat the hot milk into the egg yolks. Pour the entire mixture back into the pan and place over low heat. Stir constantly until the temperature reaches 150°F or the mixture is thick enough to coat the back of a wooden spoon. Immediately remove from heat. Strain into a large bowl and set aside to cool.

In a small bowl beat the cream until it is slightly thickened, then fold it into the cooled egg mixture. Add the brandy, rum, vanilla, and nutmeg. Stir well. Cover and refrigerate at least 4 hours. Serve ice cold in small glasses, or serve from a medium punch bowl filled with one large block of ice (page 1).

Variations

APRICOT EGGNOG Omit the brandy. Add 8 ounces apricot brandy along with the rum, vanilla, and nutmeg.

BANANA EGGNOG Omit the rum. Add 4 ounces crème de banane along with the brandy.

CHERRY EGGNOG Omit the brandy. Add 8 ounces cherry brandy along with the rum.

COCONUT EGGNOG Reduce the whole milk to 2 cups. Add 2 cups coconut milk along with the remaining whole milk. Proceed with the recipe as directed.

JAMAICAN EGGNOG Omit the gold rum. Add 4 ounces dark rum along with the brandy.

SPICED EGGNOG Omit the gold rum. Add 4 ounces spiced rum (such as Captain Morgan), ½ teaspoon ground cinnamon, ¼ teaspoon ground allspice, and ¼ teaspoon ground mace along with the vanilla and nutmeg.

Y **Zero-Proof Variation**

VIRGIN EGGNOG Omit the brandy and gold rum. Add 1½ cups orange juice and 2 teaspoons rum flavoring (optional).

GARDEN PARTY PUNCH

Bursting with fruit flavors, this punch tastes like summer in a glass.

2 cups mango nectar

1 cup black currant juice

1 cup strawberry juice (see Note below)

½ cup banana nectar

¼ cup fresh lime juice

8 ounces gold rum

2 teaspoons white crème de menthe

Fill a 2-quart pitcher three-quarters full with ice. Add all the ingredients and stir well. Serve over ice in tall glasses.

Note: Strawberry juice is available at many gourmet stores or by mail from Central Market (800-360-2552).

 **Zero-Proof Variation**

KID'S GARDEN PARTY PUNCH Omit the rum and crème de menthe. Add 1 drop peppermint extract before serving.

GLOGG

Sweet and spicy, this warm punch is perfect for your trim-a-tree party, New Year's Eve bash, or Groundhog Day celebration.

Zest of 1/2 orange

One 4-inch cinnamon stick

4 cloves

2 cardamom pods

1 bottle (750 milliliters) red wine (such as cabernet)

3 tablespoons honey

6 ounces blended whiskey

2 tablespoons raisins

1/4 cup whole almonds, toasted (see Note below)

Combine the orange zest, cinnamon, cloves, cardamom, wine, and honey in a medium saucepan. Place over medium heat until warm. Remove from the heat, cover, and let steep for 1 to 2 hours. Strain the mixture and return to the pan. Add the whiskey, raisins, and almonds. Place over low heat until the glogg is warm. Serve in mugs, making sure to include some raisins and almonds in each. Keep warm over very low heat.

Note: Toast the almonds in a skillet over medium heat for 2 to 3 minutes or until fragrant, stirring constantly.

 **Zero-Proof Variation**

CONCORD GRAPE GLOGG Omit the wine and whiskey. Add 1 quart concord grape juice to the pan with the spices, and add 3/4 cup white grape juice along with the raisins and almonds.

GROOVY BANANA WINE PUNCH

Perfect if you're throwing a retro party or if you've never left the sixties. Just keep in mind that this punch needs to "marinate" overnight.

1 bottle (750 milliliters) white wine (such as chardonnay)

1 cup orange juice

½ cup lemon juice

1 heaping cup crushed pineapple in juice (8-ounce can)

½ cup packed light brown sugar

3 bananas, peeled and sliced into 1-inch pieces

2½ cups white rum

4 ounces dark rum

6 ounces crème de banane

Combine the wine, orange juice, lemon juice, pineapple, and sugar in a large pitcher or bowl. Stir until the sugar is dissolved. Add the bananas. Cover and refrigerate for 24 hours.

Strain the mixture into a punch bowl filled halfway with ice. Discard the fruit (or save the bananas to use in banana daiquiris—but use them immediately as they won't keep). Add the white rum, dark rum, and crème de banane. Stir well. Serve in any size glass you like, up or over ice.

Variations

APPLE WINE PUNCH Omit the bananas and crème de banane. Add 4 apples, seeded and chopped, along with the pineapple. After straining, add 6 ounces apple schnapps along with the rum.

PEACH WINE PUNCH Omit the bananas and crème de banane. Add 4 peaches, sliced and pitted, along with the pineapple. After straining, add 6 ounces peach schnapps along with the rum.

PEAR WINE PUNCH Omit the bananas and crème de banane. Add 4 pears, seeded and chopped, along with the pineapple. After straining, add 6 ounces pear liqueur along with the rum.

STRAWBERRY WINE PUNCH Omit the bananas and crème de banane. Add 1 quart sliced strawberries along with the pineapple. After straining, add 6 ounces strawberry schnapps along with the rum.

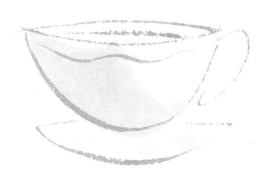

LEMONADE

MAKES ABOUT 6 CUPS

When life gives you lemons, make lemonade. When it doesn't, go out and buy them.

    1 cup lemon juice
    1 cup superfine sugar
    4½ cups water

Combine the lemon juice and sugar in a large pitcher. Stir until the sugar is completely dissolved. Add the water. Serve over ice in tall glasses.

Variations

APRICOT LEMONADE Add 2 cups apricot nectar along with the water. Makes 8 cups.

BLUEBERRY LEMONADE In a blender, puree 2 cups fresh blueberries with 3 tablespoons water and 1 tablespoon light corn syrup. Add the puree along with the water. Makes about 7½ cups.

CHERRY LEMONADE Reduce the sugar by ¼ cup. Add ¼ cup cherry syrup along with the lemon juice.

HONEY LEMONADE Omit the sugar. Add 1 cup honey to the lemon juice. Proceed with the recipe as directed.

PINEAPPLE LEMONADE Add 2 cups pineapple juice along with the water. Makes 8 cups.

PINK PLUM LEMONADE In a blender, puree 4 large, red or purple plums (sliced and pitted) with 2 tablespoons water and 1 tablespoon light corn syrup. Add the puree along with the water. Makes about 7½ cups.

RASPBERRY LEMONADE In a blender, puree 1 cup fresh raspberries with 2 tablespoons water and 1 tablespoon light corn syrup. Strain through a sieve to remove the seeds. You may need to push the mixture through with a wooden spoon. Add the puree along with the water. Makes about 7 cups.

STRAWBERRY LEMONADE In a blender, puree 1 quart strawberries, hulled and sliced, with 2 tablespoons water and 2 tablespoons light corn syrup. Add the puree along with the water. Makes about 8½ cups.

VANILLA LEMONADE Reduce the sugar by ¼ cup. Add ¼ cup vanilla syrup (available from Dean & DeLuca [212-431-1691]) along with the lemon juice.

WATERMELON LEMONADE In a blender, puree 3 cups chopped, seeded watermelon with 2 tablespoons light corn syrup. Strain to remove any bits of seeds that remain. Add the puree along with the water. Makes about 8½ cups.

Spiked Variations

LEMON DROPPER Add 2 cups vodka along with the water. Makes 8 cups.

MEXICAN LEMONADE Add 2 cups white tequila along with the water. Makes 8 cups.

PIRATE'S LEMONADE Add 2 cups white rum along with the water. Makes 8 cups.

THE QUEEN'S LEMONADE Add 2 cups gin along with the water. Makes 8 cups.

LIGHTNING JUICE PUNCH

MAKES ABOUT 2 QUARTS

This drink actually seems to glow. And that's even before you've had one or two glasses of the stuff.

> 6 ounces coconut rum (such as Malibu)
>
> 4 ounces melon liqueur (such as Midori)
>
> 4 ounces triple sec
>
> 1½ cups orange juice
>
> 1½ cups pineapple juice

Fill a large pitcher with ice. Add all the ingredients and stir well. Serve in tall glasses filled with ice.

SERVING SUGGESTION: Fill two ice-cube trays with orange juice and two trays with pineapple juice. Place in the freezer until the juice is frozen. Fill the pitcher with frozen juice cubes instead of regular ice. Juice cubes can also be used to fill the glasses.

LILLET PUNCH

Lillet is a sweet wine from France, with the flavors of orange and spice. It's available in red or white, at nearly any liquor store.

3 cups orange sherbet

8 ounces white Lillet wine

6 ounces Grand Marnier

3 ounces crème de cassis

2¼ cups orange juice

Place the orange sherbet in a 2-quart pitcher or punch bowl. Add the remaining ingredients and stir well, until the sherbet is mostly melted.

Variation

LILLET PUNCH FOR 1

1½ ounces white Lillet wine

½ ounce Grand Marnier

½ ounce crème de cassis

4 ounces orange juice

1 small scoop orange sherbet

Fill a tall iced tea glass with ice. Add all the ingredients expect the sherbet. Stir well. Top with the sherbet.

LIMEADE

MAKES ABOUT 6 CUPS

Since I often have a pitcher of both limeade and lemonade on hand, I add a few drops of green food coloring to the limeade, so I can recognize it when guests ask for a glass.

1 cup fresh lime juice

1 cup superfine sugar

4 cups water

2 drops green food coloring (optional)

Combine the lime juice and sugar in a large pitcher. Stir until the sugar is completely dissolved. Add the water and food coloring and stir. Serve over ice in tall glasses.

Variations

CREAMY COCONUT LIMEADE Increase the sugar to 1¼ cups. Add 1 cup unsweetened coconut milk along with the water. Makes 7 cups.

GINGER LIMEADE Add 2 cups ginger ale along with the water. Serve immediately as the ginger ale will go flat. Makes 8 cups.

GREEN MELON LIMEADE In a blender, puree 2 cups chopped honeydew (or other white- or green-fleshed melon) with ¼ cup water and 2 tablespoons light corn syrup. Add the puree along with the water. Makes about 8 cups.

GUAVA LIMEADE Add 1½ cups guava nectar along with the water. Makes 7½ cups.

MANGO LIMEADE Add 1½ cups mango nectar along with the water. Makes 7½ cups.

PAPAYA LIMEADE In a blender, puree 2 cups chopped papaya with ¼ cup water and 2 tablespoons light corn syrup. Add the puree to the limeade. Makes about 8 cups.

PASSION FRUIT LIMEADE Add 1 cup passion fruit juice along with the water. Makes about 7 cups.

PEACHY LIMEADE Add 2 cups peach nectar along with the water. Makes about 8 cups.

PEAR LIMEADE Add 2 cups pear nectar along with the water. Makes about 8 cups.

TROPICAL LIMEADE Reduce the water to 3 cups. Add 3 cups guanabana nectar along with the water. Makes about 8 cups.

Spiked Variations

AZTEC LIMEADE COCKTAIL Add 2 cups gold tequila along with the water. Makes about 8 cups.

COCONUT LIMEADE COCKTAIL Add 2 cups coconut rum (such as Malibu) along with the water. Makes about 8 cups.

ISLAND LIMEADE COCKTAIL Add 2 cups gold rum along with the water. Makes about 8 cups.

SIMPLE LIMEADE COCKTAIL Add 2 cups vodka along with the water. Makes about 8 cups.

MELON SHERBET PUNCH

A good way to serve this drink is to scoop your sherbet using a melon baller. This simulates tiny melon balls floating in the punch. For extra fun, add 1 to 2 cups real, frozen melon balls as well.

    2 ounces melon liqueur (such as Midori)

    2 ounces raspberry liqueur (such as Chambord or crème de framboise)

    2 ounces crème de banane

    ½ cup lemonade

    2 teaspoons grenadine syrup

    1 pint lemon sherbet (or sorbet)

    1 to 2 cups frozen melon balls (optional)

    1 cup ginger ale

Combine the melon and raspberry liqueurs, crème de banane, lemonade, and grenadine syrup in a large pitcher or punch bowl. Stir well. Add the sherbet in one large scoop, or use a melon baller to make tiny scoops and add them to the punch along with the frozen melon balls. Top with the ginger ale and stir gently.

Variations

FRENCH MELON PUNCH Use champagne instead of ginger ale.

LIME MELON PUNCH Use limeade instead of lemonade, and lemon sherbet (or sorbet) instead of lime sherbet (or sorbet).

ORANGE MELON PUNCH Use orange juice instead of lemonade, and orange sherbet instead of lemon sherbet (or sorbet).

ONE PUNCH TKO

This punch is so sweet, you'll never know what hit you. The recipe below makes one pitcher, but you can double, triple, or quadruple the ingredients—just mix them in a large punch bowl, filled halfway with ice.

- 4 ounces peach schnapps
- 4 ounces dark rum
- 2 ounces cherry liqueur (such as Heering)
- 2 ounces brandy
- 2 ounces triple sec
- 1 cup pineapple juice
- 1 cup orange juice
- 1 cup passion fruit juice
- 2 teaspoons fresh lime juice

Fill a large pitcher with ice. Add all the ingredients and stir well. Serve in tall glasses filled with ice.

PACIFIC DEEP SEA PUNCH

Have a snorkel handy, because this punch is so refreshing, your guests may want to take a dive into the punch bowl after just one glass.

3 cups lemonade

1 1/2 cups unsweetened coconut milk

12 ounces blue curaçao

6 ounces vodka

3 ounces sweetened bottled lime juice

Fill a large pitcher or punch bowl halfway with ice. Add all the ingredients and stir well. Serve in small glasses over ice.

SERVING SUGGESTION: Serve very cold, in small glasses without ice. Place one or two gummy sharks, gummy octopus, gummy worms, or Swedish fish in each glass before serving.

PIMM'S #1 CUP PUNCH

MAKES ABOUT 5 QUARTS

Pimm's is a British, gin-based liqueur, reportedly the Queen's favorite. It may seem odd to add cucumbers to a cocktail, but one learns early on never to question HRM.

1 quart strawberries, hulled and sliced

1 large cucumber, peeled, seeded, and diced

1 bottle Pimm's #1 (750 milliliters)

8 ounces gin

Juice of 4 lemons

¼ cup sugar

8 cups ice

2 cups ginger ale

Combine all the ingredients, except the ice and ginger ale, in a large punch bowl. Cover and let sit for at least 2 hours. Add the ice and ginger ale just before serving. Stir gently. Make sure each serving contains pieces of fruit, cucumber, and ice.

SERVING SUGGESTIONS AND TIPS: Peel and slice 2 cucumbers in half crosswise. Slice each half into quarters, lengthwise. Garnish each serving with one cucumber "stick."

Add any additional fruit you like, including grapes, sliced bananas, raspberries, and peaches. Freezing the fruit first will help keep the punch cold.

Variation

BRITISH PUNCH Substitute tonic water for the ginger ale.

PINK ELEPHANT PUNCH

When you start seeing pink elephants, you've had enough.

    3 cups strawberry juice (see Note below)

    1½ cups unsweetened coconut milk

    12 ounces vodka

    6 ounces almond liqueur (such as amaretto or crème de noya)

    6 ounces grenadine syrup

Fill a large pitcher or punch bowl halfway with ice. Add all the ingredients and stir well. Serve in small glasses over ice.

Note: Strawberry juice is available at many gourmet stores or by mail from Central Market (800-360-2552).

SERVING SUGGESTIONS: Fill ice-cube trays with cranberry juice cocktail and place in the freezer until frozen solid. Use the frozen juice cubes instead of regular ice.

If you are serving this in a punch bowl, 1 quart of frozen strawberries makes a nice addition. If you are using a pitcher, add a few frozen berries to each glass along with the ice.

RHUBARB ELIXIR

Since fresh rhubarb is more flavorful and colorful than commercially frozen rhubarb, I buy extra rhubarb when it's available in early spring. I slice it into ½-inch pieces and freeze it for use all year.

> 1½ pounds fresh rhubarb
>
> ¾ cup sugar
>
> Juice of ½ lime
>
> 1 drop red food coloring (optional)

Slice the rhubarb into ½-inch pieces. Place in a 3-quart saucepan and add enough water just to cover the fruit. Bring to a boil over high heat. Reduce the heat to low and simmer, covered, for 20 minutes, stirring occasionally. At this point the rhubarb should be soft enough to break apart when stirred.

Pour the mixture into a fine strainer set over a large bowl. You may also use a jelly bag to strain the mixture. Allow as much liquid as possible to drain. It's done when the dripping stops and the pulp is thick and pasty. Discard the pulp and stir the sugar into the rhubarb juice. Chill the juice in the refrigerator for at least 4 hours. Add the lime juice and food coloring to the chilled juice and pour into a pitcher. Serve over ice in tall glasses.

Note: I like to garnish this with red rock candy swizzle sticks, available by mail from Dean & DeLuca (212-431-1691).

 Variations

CINNAMON RHUBARB ELIXIR Add one 4-inch cinnamon stick to the pan along with the rhubarb. Proceed with the recipe as directed. Garnish the drinks with tall cinnamon sticks.

VANILLA RHUBARB ELIXIR Add 1 split vanilla bean to the pan along with the rhubarb. Proceed with the recipe as directed.

RHUBARB TEA PUNCH

This punch is perfect for kids or adults.

  1 quart Rhubarb Elixir (page 156)

  1 quart unsweetened, strong iced tea

  1 bottle (1 liter) lemon-lime soda (optional)

  Fresh strawberries for garnish

  Lemon wedges for garnish

Fill a large punch bowl halfway with ice. Add the Rhubarb Elixir and tea. Stir well. If desired, add the lemon-line soda just before serving. Garnish each glass with fresh strawberries and lemon wedges.

Variations

PEACH RHUBARB PUNCH Omit the iced tea. Add 1 quart peach nectar along with the Rhubarb Elixir. If desired, add a 1-liter bottle of ginger ale just before serving.

STRAWBERRY RHUBARB PUNCH Omit the iced tea. Add 1 quart strawberry juice along with the Rhubarb Elixir. If desired, add a 1-liter bottle strawberry soda just before serving. Strawberry juice is available at many gourmet stores or by mail from Central Market (800-360-2552).

Spiked Variations

RHUBARB RUMBA COCKTAIL Omit the iced tea. Add 2 cups coconut rum (such as Malibu) instead.

RUSSIAN RHUBARB PUNCH Omit the iced tea. Add 2 cups vodka and ¼ cup sweetened bottled lime juice instead.

SANGRIA #1 (FAST AND EASY)

There are several ways to make Sangria. This one is simple but tastes authentic.

1 bottle (750 milliliters) red wine (such as Spanish rioja)

4 ounces brandy

4 ounces triple sec

1/2 cup orange juice

1/4 cup lemon juice

2 cups ginger ale

2 oranges, sliced thin

2 lemons, sliced thin

Combine all the ingredients except the fruit slices in a large pitcher. Float the orange and lemon slices on top. Serve very cold over ice in tall glasses.

Variations

APPLE SANGRIA Omit the ginger ale. Add 2 cups sparkling cider (with or without alcohol) along with the other liquid ingredients.

BERRY SANGRIA Omit the triple sec and orange and lemon slices. Add 4 ounces raspberry liqueur (such as Chambord or crème de framboise) along with the other liquid ingredients. Add 1 pint sliced strawberries and 1 pint whole raspberries before serving.

CELEBRATION SANGRIA Omit the ginger ale. Add 2 cups Asti Spumante (or other sweet sparkling white wine) along with the other liquid ingredients.

SANGRIA #2 (TRADITIONAL)

This sangria requires a little planning ahead, but the results are well worth the effort.

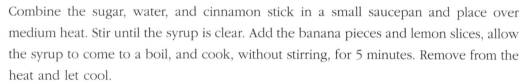

⅓ cup sugar

½ cup water

One 4-inch cinnamon stick

1 banana, peeled and broken into pieces

1 lemon, sliced thin

½ cup orange juice

1 bottle (750 milliliters) red wine (such as Spanish rioja)

2 to 3 cups sliced fruit for garnish (such as oranges, limes, and peaches)

Combine the sugar, water, and cinnamon stick in a small saucepan and place over medium heat. Stir until the syrup is clear. Add the banana pieces and lemon slices, allow the syrup to come to a boil, and cook, without stirring, for 5 minutes. Remove from the heat and let cool.

Strain the syrup through a fine sieve into a large pitcher. Add the orange juice and wine. Add the sliced fruit and stir well. Serve cold over ice in tall glasses or serve in a punch bowl with one large block of ice (page 1).

Variation

SANGRIA BLANCO Omit the red wine and orange juice. Add 1 bottle (750 milliliters) white wine (such as chardonnay) and ½ cup apple juice to the cooled syrup.

SUMMER MELON PUNCH

I always make two pitchers of this summer favorite for every party, one with alcohol and one without. To help me remember which is which, I often use yellow watermelon quencher for one punch and red watermelon quencher for the other.

> 2 cups Watermelon Quencher (page 161)
>
> 2 cups pear nectar
>
> 1 cup lychee juice (see Note below)
>
> ½ cup lemonade
>
> 6 ounces white rum
>
> 6 ounces spiced rum (such as Captain Morgan)
>
> 2 teaspoons grenadine syrup

Fill a large pitcher or punch bowl with ice. Add all the ingredients and stir well. Serve in tall glasses filled with ice.

Note: Lychee juice is available in specialty stores or by mail from Central Market (800-360-2552) or Healthy Pleasures Village (212-353-3663).

 **Zero-Proof Variation**

BUZZ-FREE SUMMER MELON PUNCH Omit both kinds of rum. Add 1½ cups white grape juice instead.

WATERMELON QUENCHER

You can make this from any color watermelon, as long as it's fresh and sweet.

5 cups roughly chopped watermelon, yellow or red (seeds removed)

1/4 cup superfine sugar

Juice of 1 lime

Place all the ingredients in a blender. Cover and blend until the fruit is liquefied. Pour through a strainer into a large pitcher. Allow the mixture to drain without pushing it through the strainer. Discard any solids that remain. Skim any remaining foam from the juice and serve over ice in tall glasses.

Variations

BASIL WATERMELON COOLER Add 6 fresh basil leaves before blending.

MINTY WATERMELON COOLER Add 2 to 3 sprigs fresh mint before blending.

TARRAGON WATERMELON COOLER Add 2 tablespoons chopped fresh tarragon before blending.

ZINGY WATERMELON COOLER Add 1 to 2 teaspoons hot pepper sauce before blending.

Spiked Variations

FRENCH WATERMELON COCKTAIL Add 4 ounces crème de cassis to the pitcher before serving.

JAMAICAN WATERMELON COCKTAIL Add 6 ounces gold rum to the pitcher before serving.

RUSSIAN WATERMELON COCKTAIL Add 6 ounces vodka to the pitcher before serving.

WATERMELON MARGARITA Add 4 ounces tequila, 4 ounces triple sec, 3 ounces sweetened bottled lime juice to the pitcher before serving.

YOUNGBERRY PUNCH

Youngberries look like a cross between raspberries and blackberries, but taste sweeter than both. Youngberry juice (along with strawberry juice and papaya nectar) is available in many gourmet stores or by mail from Central Market (800-360-2552) or Healthy Pleasures Village (212-353-3663).

2 cups youngberry juice

2 cups papaya nectar

1 cup strawberry juice

4 ounces lemon liqueur (such as Limoncello)

4 ounces brandy

Combine all the ingredients in a pitcher. Chill well and pour over ice in tall glasses.

 Zero-Proof Variation

YOUNGSTER'S YOUNGBERRY PUNCH Simply omit the brandy and Limoncello. Serve over ice in tall glasses. Makes about 5 cups.

SERVING SUGGESTIONS: Fill ice-cube trays with youngberry juice and freeze until solid. Serve the punch over youngberry ice cubes instead of regular ice.

If desired, top with a scoop of lime sherbet or lime sorbet and a splash of ginger ale.

ZOMBIES FOR A CROWD

This punch should be served with plenty of ice—and plenty to eat.

12 ounces white rum

12 ounces dark rum

4 ounces orange curaçao (or triple sec)

4 ounces apricot brandy or apricot liqueur (such as Apry)

2½ cups orange juice

2½ cups pineapple juice

1 cup lemon juice

2 tablespoons almond syrup

Combine all the ingredients in a large container and set aside. Fill a large punch bowl three-quarters full with ice. Add half the punch and stir well. As the punch runs down, add more ice and more punch. Or you can serve this punch from a pitcher filled with ice.

Variation

ZOMBIE FOR 1

¾ ounce white rum

¾ ounce dark rum

¼ ounce triple sec

¼ ounce apricot liqueur (such as Apry)

1½ ounces pineapple juice

1½ ounces orange juice

½ ounce lemon juice

1 teaspoon almond syrup

Fill a cocktail shaker three-quarters full with ice. Add all the ingredients, cover, and shake well. Strain over fresh ice in a tall glass.

TODDIES

HOT CHOCOLATE, COFFEE, JUICE, AND TEA DRINKS

HOT CHOCOLATE TODDIES

All of these drinks can be made with packaged hot cocoa mix or homemade (page 169).

Technique: Add all the ingredients to a warm mug, in the order listed. Each recipe makes 1 drink.

CHOCOCHERRY

1 ounce dark rum

1 ounce cherry syrup

1/2 ounce dark crème de cacao

Hot cocoa to fill mug

COCOBERRY

1 ounce coconut rum (such as Malibu)

1 ounce raspberry liqueur (such as Chambord or crème de framboise)

Hot cocoa to fill mug

DOUBLE CINNAMON COCOA

2 ounces dark crème de cacao

1/2 ounce cinnamon schnapps

Hot cocoa to fill mug

JUNGLE COCOA

1 ounce crème de banane

1 ounce white crème de cacao

Hot cocoa to fill mug

VANILLA COCOA

1 ounce vanilla liqueur (such as Licor 43)

1 ounce brandy

Hot cocoa to fill mug

ZERO-PROOF CHOCOLATE STEAMERS

CHOCOLATE NUT

2 tablespoons unsweetened

coconut milk

1 tablespoon almond-flavored

syrup

Hot cocoa to fill mug

Whipped cream and chopped

nuts for topping

CHOCOLATE MINT
DREAM

Hot cocoa to fill mug three-

quarters full

1 scoop mint chip ice cream

for topping

HOT VANILLA
CHOCOLATE

2 tablespoons vanilla syrup

Hot cocoa to fill mug

Whipped cream and white

chocolate chips for

topping

HOT COCOA FROM SCRATCH

2 tablespoons sugar

2 tablespoons cocoa powder

1 cup milk (regular, low-fat, or non-fat)

Mix the sugar and cocoa powder in a mug. Bring the milk to a simmer in a small heavy saucepan. Pour the hot milk into the mug and stir well.

HOT COFFEE TODDIES

All of these drinks are best served in large mugs that can keep the drink warm. You can also prewarm your mugs by filling them with hot (not boiling) water while you brew the coffee.

Technique: Add all the ingredients to a warm mug, in the order listed. Each recipe makes 1 drink.

ALPINE COFFEE

1 ounce almond liqueur (such as crème de noya or amaretto)

½ ounce Grand Marnier

Hot coffee to fill mug

1 scoop butter pecan ice cream for topping

COFFEE CANDY

1 ounce butterscotch schnapps

1 ounce vanilla liqueur (such as Licor 43)

1 ounce coffee liqueur (such as Kahlúa)

Hot coffee to fill mug

1 scoop coffee ice cream for topping

FRENCH TRUFFLE

1½ ounces brandy

1 ounce dark crème de cacao

Hot coffee to fill mug

Whipped cream for topping

GEORGIA BROWN

1 ounce peach schnapps

1 ounce hazelnut liqueur (such as Frangelico)

Hot coffee to fill mug

Whipped cream for topping

IRISH COFFEE

1½ ounces Irish whiskey

1 ounce Irish cream liqueur

(such as Baileys)

Hot coffee to fill mug

Whipped cream for topping

MEXICAN JUMPING
BEAN

2 ounces coffee liqueur (such as

Kahlúa)

½ ounce cinnamon schnapps

Hot coffee to fill mug

Whipped cream for topping

SICILIAN DREAMS

2 ounces anise liqueur (such as

sambuca or Pernod)

Hot coffee to fill mug

Lemon twist for garnish

SKI SLOPE

1 ounce white crème de menthe

1½ ounces white crème de

cacao

1 ounce heavy cream

Hot coffee to fill mug

Peppermint stick for garnish

COFFEE CARAMEL MELT

2 tablespoons caramel topping

Hot coffee to fill mug

Whipped cream for topping

COFFEE OVERLOAD

2 tablespoons coffee syrup

Hot coffee to fill mug three-
quarters full

1 scoop coffee ice cream for
topping

RASPBERRY COFFEE CAKE

1 tablespoon hazelnut syrup

1 tablespoon raspberry syrup

Hot coffee to fill mug

Whipped cream for topping

SWEET MOCHA DREAMS

2 tablespoons chocolate syrup

Hot coffee to fill mug three-
quarters full

1 scoop chocolate ice cream
for topping

HOT JUICE TODDIES

To make each one of these, you'll need to warm the juice first. You can do this in a small pan over low heat or in the microwave.

Technique: Add all the ingredients to a warm mug, in the order listed. Each recipe makes 1 drink.

APPLES AND ORANGES

1 1/2 ounces brandy

1 ounce triple sec

Hot apple juice to fill mug

CHRISTMAS HEAT

1 ounce triple sec

1/2 ounce vodka

1/2 ounce cinnamon schnapps

Hot apple juice to fill mug

GOLDEN DELICIOUS

1 ounce gold rum

1 ounce ginger liqueur (such as the Original Canton)

Hot apple juice to fill mug

HOT APPLE PIE

1 ounce vodka

1 ounce cinnamon

schnapps

Hot apple juice to fill mug

LEMONS AND HONEY

1 1/2 ounces citrus vodka

1/2 ounce honey liqueur (such

as Bärenjäger)

Hot cranberry juice to fill mug

ONE HOT HAWAIIAN

1 ounce coconut rum (such as

Malibu)

1 ounce gold rum

Hot pineapple juice to fill mug

Ground cinnamon and ground

nutmeg for sprinkling

PORT IN A STORM

2 ounces port wine

1/2 ounce blackberry brandy

Hot cranberry juice to fill mug

TOO HOT BERRIES

1 ounce crème de cassis

1 1/2 ounces gold rum

Hot cranberry juice to fill mug

ZERO-PROOF JUICE SOOTHERS

CRANBERRY ORANGE SPICE

2 tablespoons orange juice
concentrate, thawed

1/8 teaspoon ground cinnamon

2 cloves

Hot cranberry juice to fill mug

HONEY LICORICE LEMON DROP

2 tablespoons honey

1/8 teaspoon ground anise seed

Hot lemonade to fill mug

WARM APPLE STRUDEL

1 tablespoon almond-flavored
syrup

1/8 teaspoon ground cinnamon

Hot apple cider to fill mug

WARM CARIBBEAN BREEZE

1/4 cup banana nectar

1 teaspoon sweetened cream
of coconut

Hot pineapple juice to fill mug

HOT TEA TODDIES

Unless otherwise specified, use non-herbal tea when making these drinks.

Technique: Add all the ingredients to a warm mug, in the order listed. Each recipe makes 1 drink.

BAKED APPLE

1 1/2 ounces vodka

1 1/2 ounces apple schnapps

Hot apple spice tea (or regular tea) to fill mug

BEEHIVE

1 ounce gold rum

1 ounce honey liqueur (such as Bärenjäger)

Hot tea to fill mug

BLACK FOREST TEA

1 ounce honey liqueur (such as Bärenjäger)

1 1/2 ounces currant-flavored vodka

Hot tea to fill mug

HOT BUTTERED HAZELNUT RUM TEA

1 ounce hazelnut liqueur (such as Frangelico)

1 ounce gold rum

2 teaspoons brown sugar

1/2 teaspoon butter

Hot tea to fill mug

VERMONT NIGHTS

1 1/2 ounces peach brandy

1/2 ounce maple syrup

Hot tea to fill mug

ZERO-PROOF TEA DRINKS

APPLE CHAMOMILE TEA

2 tablespoons frozen apple juice concentrate, thawed

Hot chamomile tea to fill mug

Tall cinnamon stick for garnish

PINEAPPLE LEMON TEA

2 tablespoons frozen pineapple juice concentrate, thawed

Hot Lemon Zinger tea to fill mug

RASPBERRY LEMON ZINGER

2 tablespoons raspberry syrup

Juice of $1/2$ lemon

Hot Red Zinger tea to fill mug

TROPICAL DREAMS

2 tablespoons passion fruit syrup

$1/4$ teaspoon ground ginger

Hot green tea to fill mug

INDEX